THE CARROT CHASER

PRAISE FOR THE CARROT CHASER

"I was hooked early in the book and felt connected to the characters. The style of writing was very enjoyable and the subtle lessons throughout the book were very applicable. Todd and Ray did a great job of articulating so much of the way life works and situations I have experienced. I am looking forward to sharing the book with many family and friends."

> Mary Miller
> CEO, Jancoa
> Co-creator of The Dream Manager
> Cincinnati, Ohio

"Simple, yet profound, The Carrot Chaser weaves practical Bible principals into an exciting love story that you just can't put down."

> Dr. Mike French,
> Pensacola, FL

"A wonderful example of the trials, tribulations and choices we all face. The Carrot Chaser is a captivating story of failure and restoration in todays busy world. Todd Hopkins and Ray Hilbert deliver four truths that will change your life."

> Mark White
> Publisher
> Panhandle Publishing

"The creative style C.S. Lewis used to deliver critical truth through engaging and entertaining stories lives through this remarkable book. If you desire to trust Him more fully then you need to carve out a couple hours to immerse yourself in this story. You will be refreshed and rewarded through the Carrot Chaser story and it will be one of the books you too recommend."

Jerrod Sessler
CEO
HomeTask.com
Seattle, WA

"This book could not be more timely. With the world today so fixated on material possession, fame, and fortune, 'The Carrot Chaser' powerfully exhorts us to keep our priorities in order and to stop chasing carrots that can destroy our work, our families, and our testimonies."

Dr. Jim Harris
Award-winning Author, Speaker,
& International Consultant

"Cudos to Todd Hopkins and Ray Hilbert. 'The Janitor' was great and 'The Carrot Chaser'- is even better, of the same caliber as Og Mandino's works."

Stan Carver
..a church pew friend

"WOW. The Carrot Chaser is a must read. A simple story with profound depth... This book clearly shows that God's simple truths are available to anyone who believes in putting Him first in your personal and business life."

Michael D'Arezzo
Director, Franchise Sales
CKE Restaurants, Inc., Carl's Jr.
Carpinteria, CA

"This is a book all young inspiring men should read whether you are starting a business, a career or family. A story of how God works with us through our trust and doubt."

> Andrew T. Smart
> President and CEO
> Duke Sandwich Inc.
> Greenville, SC

"Carrot Chaser is a must read for anyone who is interested in a challenging yet fun read packed full of wisdom and insight. It is a practical account of decisions and choices we face on a daily basis. This book illustrates through the four truths that God can, wants to, and will do more than we could ever hope for or imagine on our own, if we allow him to by being receptive to and responsive to his whispers. I love how Todd and Ray illustrate God's goodness to us through Matthew. I really enjoyed this book and the practical truths that are laid out between the pages challenged me to believe God in all things."

> Steve Smith
> Office Pride Area Developer
> Visalia, CA

"Thanks to *The Carrot Chaser*, anyone can read and learn the powerful truths for honoring God in their work that Todd Hopkins and Ray Hilbert have been teaching the Office Pride and Truth@Work families for years. These truths are sure to change your life, as they have mine."

> Mark Charles
> Office Pride Area Developer
> Pensacola, FL

TODD HOPKINS & RAY HILBERT

THE CARROT CHASER
TRUTHS

TRUTH#1
**We must choose
God's agenda instead of our own.**

TRUTH#2
We must recognize the carrots.

TRUTH#3
We must not try to put God in a box.

TRUTH#4
**We must follow God on His plan,
not include Him in ours.**

THE CARROT CHASER

Published in Pensacola, Florida by At The Cross Publishing.

At The Cross Publishing titles may be purchased in bulk for educational, business, fund-raising, or ministry use. For information, please contact the authors or visit www.the-janitorbook.com

Printed in the United States of America
10 9 8 7 6 5 4 3 2
First Edition

Front cover artwork and design by John Hamilton.

TODD HOPKINS & RAY HILBERT

THE CARROT CHASER

4 TRUTHS FOR LIVING OUT YOUR FAITH AT HOME AND IN THE MARKETPLACE

TODD HOPKINS & RAY HILBERT

*Dedicated to all the business people out there
who do the right things for the right reasons.
May God bless you greatly.*

PRESENTED TO

_____

BY

_____

ON THIS DATE

_____

FOREWORD

Once again, Hopkins & Hilbert have written a book that packs a wallop without hitting you over the head. It's so easy for professionals today to get caught on that "slippery slope" of performance and achievement. No one wants to wake up one day and realize that their spouse is a distant acquaintance, their kids don't like them, and their friends have drifted away. The Carrot Chaser is a great reminder to keep our priorities straight, and, perhaps more importantly, a reminder that we all need someone a little bit ahead of us in the game to reach back and help us avoid the pitfalls they've already experienced.

Not since The Janitor have I read a book that uses the power of allegory to make such a timeless and important set of lessons come to life. This book will change the way you look at, well, everything!

Brett Clemmer
Vice President
Man In The Mirror
Orlando, Florida

CHAPTER ONE

BALANCING ONE TALL, SKIM LATTE IN EACH HAND, Matthew Swift nimbly swerved across the crowded coffee shop back to where Michelle had found a table by the window. In the soft afternoon light, her silky hair cascaded down her slender back like a sunset on a wide golden beach. Matthew breathed in the aromatic coffee and basked in the warmth of Michelle's smile.

"Thanks, babe," she said in that bubbly voice that made Matthew think that there was no better sound in the world. "I've been meaning to ask you, have you got plans for Friday night?"

"Not really. I'll probably work right through the weekend

setting up the new store," Matthew said. "The guys doing the signs are behind. Actually, I was planning on recruiting you to help . . . why?"

"Oh, nothing." Michelle shrugged and sipped her coffee. "It's okay if you're busy."

The way Michelle never made a fuss of little things was one of her endearing traits. It always surprised Matthew, ever since Michelle came into his life about seven months ago, that his once self-absorbed life was now centered on making this beautiful creature happy.

"Is there something you wanted to do?" Matthew asked, brushing off a dot of foam from her upper lip.

"My parents are celebrating their thirtieth wedding anniversary," Michelle said. "It's a last-minute thing, very informal."

"Thirty years." Matthew whistled softly. "And they invited me?" This was the "meet the parents" step, one of the many unspoken levels that move a relationship forward. He had hoped Michelle would introduce him, since he didn't want to ask. Having no parents alive, he could not take the initiative by introducing her to his.

"It's not a formal party," Michelle said. "They threw it together last minute for their closest friends and family. Dad's business caused him to be too busy to celebrate their twenty-fifth, so he promised Mom he would do something special for number thirty."

"Sounds like fun," Matthew said, grinning.

"Are you sure?" Michelle flashed her light-filled smile.

"Looking forward to it already." Matthew slapped the table playfully.

"You are a star," Michelle said, blowing a kiss across the table. "My parents are gonna love you."

"You still have to help me with the store," Matthew said. "No getting out of that one, m'lady."

"Maybe," Michelle said, "if you get me a muffin. I'm starving."

"What kind?" Matthew said.

"Banana-nut?"

"Coming right up," said Matthew, and he braved the crowd on the way back to the counter.

Michelle reached for a newspaper someone had left folded neatly on the window ledge and idly flipped through the back pages. She stopped at one article in the business section. Michelle started reading the column with increasing interest until she was literally glued to every word. When Matthew returned with her muffin, she didn't lift her head as she read the closing paragraph.

"Have you seen this?" Michelle pointed at the article.

"I never read that paper," Matthew said as his eyes made contact with the Brian Brighton-style article. "It's mostly gossip mongering that passes as business journalism."

"I think you should read it," Michelle said.

"What's it about?" Matthew noticed the slight edge on Michelle's voice.

"Does Swift Sports ring a bell?" Michelle asked.

Matthew reached for the newspaper, took a long look at the article, and started reading aloud.

SO WHAT HAS BECOME OF THAT RISING STAR?

by Brian Brighton . . . "Yours Truly"

As my faithful readers know, one of Yours Truly's most perverse hobbies is to go back in time and see what became of the fastest-rising stars of the business scene from some time ago. Did they fulfill their promise, or did they fizzle away unremarkably like yesterday's flat warm soda? Here's a case that you'll enjoy. Three years ago Matthew Swift graced the cover of business and trade magazines as one of the youngest and most talented entrepreneurs of our age. He was hailed as having one of the most brilliant young minds in the emerging business world, period. The young man, who had barely turned 28, had just taken his five-year-old venture public and cashed in for a cool $20 million, retaining the top job at the helm of the new corporation. To the naked eye, the man had it all. Matthew Swift had the money, the power, and the toys that came with it—the penthouse, the German convertible, and the giggling debutantes milling around endlessly. Sigh. I'd be jealous if I didn't know how the story developed.

Swift attempted to lead the public corporation with the same cavalier attitude with which he had grown his business from scratch. But leading a multinational sport-merchandising business requires an entirely different set of skills. While Swift was quick on his feet and could charm the feathers off a duck, he lacked other qualities, like strategy, long-term planning, and leadership. A series of greedy, over-confident decisions landed Swift at odds with the board of directors. Suppliers balked, and distributors fled. Swift Sports started to spiral into despair and debt. The rest is history. The company fired its own creator, who in a flashy (and frankly embarrassing) display of bravado, cashed out his stock at the worst possible moment and took himself out of the equation without any opportunity to profit from the eventual recovery of (the now Swiftless) Swift Sports . . .

Matthew stopped reading halfway through the article. He folded the newspaper with a slap and took a long gulp from his coffee.

"I can't believe it," he finally said. "I mean, this reporter was constantly on my case, and now, after all these years, he has to dig up all this crap? Don't they have anything else to write about?"

"Why didn't you tell me about this?" Michelle asked.

"I told you I owned a business before," Matthew said, confused.

"But you didn't say it was called Swift Sports!" Michelle said.

"Well, it's not a particularly pleasant subject," Matthew said. "Not exactly a good pick-up line. 'Hey, gorgeous, I just got fired from my own company, making me the most resounding business failure in the whole world. Wanna go out on a date with me?'"

"But we've known each other for over six months now," Michelle said, "and it never came up."

"We did talk about how my previous business had failed," he said, "and how I was making a new beginning with Easy Mattress."

Matthew couldn't peel his eyes away from the article.

"I can't believe this guy," he repeated. "Plus, he got it all wrong."

"Matthew . . . was it that bad?"

Matthew bit his upper lip. "It wasn't easy."

Michelle looked at Matthew's hands wrapped tightly around his empty cup.

"You look really upset," she said softly. "Even after such a long time, it still bothers you so much?"

"It's just . . ." he said, "something I would really like to put behind me. This guy makes a career out of digging up dirt. He feeds off other people's misery. If he knows so much about business, how come he's working as a small-fry writer? Maybe if he tried to start a business he'd discover a thing or two. It's not as easy as it looks." He paused. "Enough of that. He can boil his own head. Let's talk about something fun. Do you have to go back to the bookshop?"

"No, I'm done for today," she said. "Yannik is going to close the shop today."

"That's nice of him," Matthew said with a smirk.

"Yes, it is," she said. "He's helping me out a lot."

"I wonder why?" he said. "It's not the pay, for sure . . . Let's see . . . what could possibly interest an educated, successful PhD candidate to work in a Christian bookshop for charity-level pay? Let's see . . . what could interest him? I know . . . *you*!"

"Matthew, don't be silly," Michelle laughed. "There's nothing to be jealous of. He's just helping me get the bookstore going, and the job gives him plenty of time to study. Yannik's come up with a brilliant idea to hold small seminars with a local author who's a professor he knows from his university and specializes in life-coaching."

"I don't get that," Matthew interrupted. "What is a life coach, anyway?"

"You know . . ." she coaxed, "a professional that helps you realize your full potential."

"Sounds like a snake-oil salesman to me," he said.

"A lot of executives embrace coaching. It gives them somebody to measure their progress against, someone neutral—you know how everybody lives such a rushed life today.

Yannik said that it will bring people to the store. He says that once people see what a great job we do at the bookshop they'll keep coming back. Isn't that brilliant?"

"Fantastic," Matthew grumbled. "Yannik is a genius."

"Oh, come on," Michelle said, "you know there's only one place in my heart, and that's all filled up with you."

Matthew looked up at her eagerly. She had said what he needed most to hear.

"I love you," she said.

"I love you more."

Easy warmth flowed between them, a familiar rhythm of smiles and caring gestures that had become their life together and for the first time had given Matthew a glimpse into a future he had never dared hope for himself.

"But Matthew?" she said with a cloud in her eyes.

"Yes?" Matthew had never seen her look this foreboding before.

"I think there's something I better tell you," Michelle said. "It's about the article. Since you are going to meet my parents on Friday, I think I better tell you."

Matthew waited for her to continue.

Michelle shook her head. "You're not going to believe this. Maybe you should read the rest of the article first."

CHAPTER TWO

EVERY TIME HE PULLED INTO HIS DRIVEWAY IN A PEACEful state of mind, which lately was most of the time for Charles White, he gave thanks for his charmed life. He parked his late-model car in the garage and walked across the tidy front lawn to the generous entrance of his ample two-story home. He could go in the back door through the covered patio, but he would much rather enjoy the welcome that the neat rows of flowers and trimmed bushes offered, book-ended by two magnificent willow trees. The afternoon dew on the late-summer blooms gave off the fragrant promise of a relaxing evening. Charles White knew very well that he lived a life of infinite blessings. As he entered, the faint aroma of baking greeted him from the kitchen, where Anna was getting dinner ready.

"How is the prettiest gal in the world?" He greeted her with a kiss and a soft squeeze around her shoulders.

"Hi, honey," Anna said, meeting his kiss. "Dinner's ready if you want to wash up. Could you tell Ben to come down?"

"I'll be back in two minutes," Charles said, and slapped a folded newspaper on the table. "I brought this to show you. Read that article; you'll get a good giggle."

While Charles went upstairs to freshen up and call their son, Ben, for dinner, Anna tossed the salad and set the asparagus quiche on the table. It was so nice to have Ben home from college; he was so joyfully annoying. Their eldest daughter was already independent, with her own store and rented studio apartment. They still saw each other regularly, but the feeling of having Ben sleeping upstairs in his bedroom reminded her of the days when their house was full of wonderful noise. She leaned against the kitchen counter and picked up the article.

As the three sat at the table, Anna marveled at her son's wholesome looks. He wasn't handsome in a conventional way, but more in the way that his confidence and kindness complemented his tall, slender looks. He had the same cheerful manner as his father, but while Charles sometimes felt the weight of the world on his shoulders, Ben had a way of taking things in stride and making even his excellent grades look natural, as if he had put no effort into any of his achievements.

"Did you read the article?" Charles asked Anna. "You remember the guy, don't you?"

"What's it about?" Ben asked, heaping salad on his plate.

"It happened a few years ago, a man your dad knew," Anna started.

"'Collided with' is more like it. It's about a young man who got too big for his britches," Charles said, "and caused me a lot of grief in the process. I guess you were still in high school, Ben. Do you remember all that trouble?"

"Vaguely," Ben replied with a wink to his mother. "I remember you being grumpy all the time."

"That boy was so young," said Anna, "and success came almost too quickly, don't you think? I hope he has had the opportunity to get back on his feet."

"Well," Charles said, "he had it coming, I tell you. I hope he learned his lesson that there's some things money can't buy . . . like integrity and dignity."

"Don't get upset, honey." Anna smiled. "It'll give you indigestion."

"You're right," Charles said. "This quiche is delicious, by the way."

"Can I help you with anything for the party, Mom?" Ben asked.

The conversation turned to logistics, and Anna handed

out each of their responsibilities. The family entertained frequently and had evolved into a well-rehearsed team. Ben would take care of the music, pick up the grandparents, and arrange the fairy lights and folding tables on the patio. Anna would coordinate the catering and flowers. Charles would be in charge of the beverages and greeting guests at the door. Ben had also secretly conspired to coordinate the entrance of Charles's surprise for Anna. Since the party had been planned around the theme of their honeymoon in Mexico, with food and decorations to match, Charles had asked Ben to secretly arrange for a Mariachi band to serenade her with their favorite songs from that time. Since their honeymoon had been brief and on a strict budget, Charles was determined to make this party special. Ben was also conspiring with his sister for a surprise of their own. They had both sat for a portrait with a local artist, something their parents had expressed a wish for but had never gotten around to. The wedding anniversary was the perfect opportunity, and the artist was setting the portrait in a beautiful frame and had even included in the background of the painting a collage of signs and reminders of many of their favorite activities they did as a family while growing up.

"Are you bringing a lady friend?" Charles asked Ben playfully.

"Yes, Dad, I might bring a friend from school," Ben said, "so you can embarrass me with anecdotes from my childhood."

"Just a friend, huh?" Charles prodded.

"Dad!"

"When have I ever embarrassed you?" Charles pouted.

"Never!" Anna said, giggling as Ben rolled his eyes.

"Never? Then there's always a first time!" Charles chuckled out loud. "I'll think of something."

"I think Michelle might bring her boyfriend," Anna said casually.

"Oh?" Charles looked up, surprised.

"I think it's getting serious this time." Anna nodded and smiled to herself. "I think he might be *the one*."

"Well, there's no rush," Charles said. "She's so young."

"I was already married at her age," Anna said.

"That was different in those days."

"Sure," Anna smiled. "Promise you won't give this young man a hard time?"

Charles looked toward Ben and narrowed his eyes. "You've met him?"

"Briefly," Ben replied. "They drove me to the airport once."

Ben got up and started clearing the table.

"And?" Charles asked as Ben started loading the dishwasher.

"He's cool," Ben said with one firm nod of his head.

"You can see for yourself on Friday," Anna said. "If Michelle picked him, then he must be a lovely man. It's the first time for her to bring a boyfriend home."

"What does he do for a living?" Charles asked.

"He owns a mattress store," Ben said. "It's doing well and

is starting to expand. They're opening a second store soon on Southport Road."

"He's a young entrepreneur then," Charles said.

Ben nodded. "You could say that, yes."

"As long as he didn't learn his trade from Matthew Swift," Charles huffed.

"Oh, Charles, don't start again," Anna said.

"What do you mean?" Ben asked.

"Matthew Swift." Charles nodded toward the paper lying on the counter. "The little snot I was telling you about. The one in the article."

Ben picked up the newspaper. As he read the article, his face turned from a placid neutrality to a frown of concentration, particularly during the second half, where his father had been quoted.

. . . Trying to locate the failed entrepreneur, I came across one of his former main suppliers, who, by the way, is still happily trading with Swift Sports to this day.

"The guy was so arrogant that he almost took my company under," says Charles White, CEO of Fan Stuff, makers of specialized sports team promotional items. "He started with big promises, but when the pan hit the fire, all he would do was keep cutting down our margins until he was driving all the oxygen out of our operation. He didn't seem to care that our employees had families to feed and I had promises to keep. All he cared about

was Matthew Swift. I tried to tell him that if he kept burning so many bridges he'd eventually catch his own pants on fire. And he did. He's nothing but a carrot chaser."

In order to write a balanced account of this story, I tried to locate some of Swift's friends, but I couldn't find any. Maybe the "friends" that surrounded him when he was at the top only cared for the reflected glory and not so much about the human being. So, how could one man rise so quickly to fame and fortune only to let it all get away?

"Overconfidence and greed," says White. "In the beginning he impressed me as an alert young man, but in the end he could not be trusted. He did not care about people. His poor decision making was costly to many small businesses, and it could have been the end of mine too, if he had lasted for another three months or so. What can I say? It all finally caught up with him."

Being a pure-bred entrepreneur, Swift soon found it difficult to sit on his capital, and he set out to prove the directors had been wrong to fire him by creating a competitor. Allowing anger and frustration to be his guide, Swift began spending his capital foolishly. Within eight months, he was broke and out of the picture entirely. Where is Swift today? Yours Truly was unable to reach him, but rumor has it that . . . you guessed it . . . he is starting yet another business. At the last sighting, he was

spotted shoving a heavy bed mattress into the back of a
pickup truck . . . and that's the last we have heard of
Matthew Swift. Or is it?

Could it be? Michelle's boyfriend's name was Matthew
Swift. It could be a coincidence. But what about the mention
of the mattresses? That was Matthew's new business. It had
to be him. What were the odds of Michelle dating his father's
nemesis? Did she know? He doubted it. Michelle would have
mentioned something. Ben had a close relationship with his
sister, and they had always found it easy to talk to each other.

"What do you think?" Charles said, nodding toward the
paper.

Ben took his time to answer, not wanting to let the cat out
of the bag before he could be certain.

He shrugged. "I don't know. This 'Yours Truly' column
sounds a little cheesy."

"I can't argue with you there—wouldn't hold my breath
for a Pulitzer," Charles said. "But cheesy or not, he made my
day. I hope I never see that Matthew Swift again. The mere
thought of him almost makes me lose my appetite."

Oh boy. This is going to be interesting, Ben thought.

CHAPTER THREE

A CONSTELLATION OF FAIRY LIGHTS TWINKLED IN THE fading twilight, and music and conversation wafted into focus as Matthew and Michelle approached the White home.

"This isn't a good time to meet your folks," Matthew said, stopping at the front porch. "It's a special day for your family, and I don't want my presence to sour the party for everybody."

"I spoke with my dad, and he's fine with it," Michelle said. "Really."

Michelle had indeed spoken to her father, but his response had been far from enthusiastic. The knowledge that, by an irreverent twist of fate, his daughter was dating his former business nemesis had punched him in the gut. He had agreed to keep cool and attempt to be civil if Michelle decided to show up with the offender. Michelle had recruited her mother's help to smooth things over and try to reacquaint the former adversaries in a more positive way. Michelle thought that her father should let matters rest since they didn't have any business dealings anymore. The anniversary party was as good an opportunity as she could hope for, she thought, since her dad would be on his best behavior surrounded by his friends and family.

"I'm really not sure about this," Matthew insisted. "I think I should come back at some other time."

Too late. The double door opened wide, and there, standing with arms wide open, was Charles White sweeping Michelle into a bear hug. Michelle made a gesture toward Matthew.

"Dad, this is Matthew," she said with an additional shade of brightness in her voice.

"Yes," Charles nodded and shook hands, "we've met." He couldn't believe he was even letting this "carrot chaser" into his house. "Carrot Chaser" was the label Charles had so emotionally given Matthew as he complained about him over the years.

At that moment, another batch of guests arrived, and Michelle moved Matthew toward the patio. Michelle introduced him with a sweeping hello to everyone. Ben joined them, carrying two glasses of champagne.

"Here," he said to Matthew, and pushed a glass into his hand. "The worst is over."

Matthew felt a light tap on his shoulder and turned around to face Anna smiling broadly.

"We are really glad you came," Anna said. "It makes the day even more special. Make yourself at home and have fun."

"You have a beautiful home," Matthew said, allowing his shoulders to relax.

An impeccably dressed tall young man, with glistening black hair and an exotic, carved profile joined them.

"Yannik!" Anna said with delight. "You look dapper tonight!"

The apparition shook hands with everyone and pecked Michelle on the cheek.

"Thank you!" he replied glancing into Michelle's eyes. "And you look ravishing as usual."

After the usual pleasant small talk, the conversation between Anna, Michelle, and Yannik quickly turned to details about the life-coaching seminars at the bookstore.

"Let me rescue you," Ben said to Matthew, leading him with his hand lightly on his shoulder. "I'll show you around the house." He led Matthew through the patio doors and into the elegant living room. They took a quick tour of the adjoining dining room, kitchen, family room, and entertainment room, finally ending up in an ample office.

"This is Dad's office," Ben announced.

The far side of the room was dominated by a floor-to-ceiling window that opened to a view of the willow tree and manicured lawn in the front yard. Through the window, they could see an orange and yellow van pulling up.

"Oops!" Ben said. "That must be the band. I have to sneak them through the back door before Mom sees them. Don't move; I'll be back here in a second."

Matthew turned to follow Ben out of the room, just as Charles came in.

"Ben," Charles said, "the musicians are here."

"I'm on my way," Ben replied over his shoulder as he sprinted outside. "I was just showing Matthew around."

"I'll do the honors." Charles smiled at Matthew.

The other three walls of the office were lined in mahogany shelves displaying an enormous collection of books and glittering trophies and other sports memorabilia. Matthew showed his appreciation as Charles guided him through a few of his favorites.

"Look here." Charles opened the lock on a glass case containing a slightly faded baseball card sandwiched between two plates of lucite. "Do you know this one?"

Matthew recognized one of the ultimate jewels of sports memorabilia, the rare T-206 tobacco card picturing Honus Wagner, shortstop for the Pittsburgh Pirates from 1900 to 1917.

"Who would think of pairing tobacco and sports today, huh?" Charles said, "Apparently Wagner was not happy about it either, and he had his card pulled. Pretty modern thinking, right? So there's only about fifty of these going around. This is the best preserved one."

Matthew whistled appreciatively. "That must be worth a packet."

"I suppose . . ." Charles paused, as if considering the fact, "if you think in those terms. I see a piece of history, an athlete who was able to stand up for what he believed was right. A statement of the integrity of the human spirit. Not everything can be measured in money. There's other things that are important to me, you know?"

"I didn't mean to say that money was its only value," Matthew said.

"It's just that I feel strongly about this." Charles's neck began to flush. "I think today people are inclined to measure everything in financial terms and they are missing the bigger equation. Money has its place, but it is just one part of it."

"But I find," said Matthew, "that people who say that money is not everything are those who have a lot of it."

Charles did a double take, as if he could not believe what he had just heard.

An awkward pause followed, and Matthew diverted his attention to a second collection of team merchandising, mugs, banners, and helmets.

"Those are some of Fan Stuff's products," Charles said, "but you are already familiar with those."

Matthew nodded.

"Listen, Matthew," Charles said, "I'd better clear the air.

You know I didn't agree with the way you conducted business."

Charles paused to gather his thoughts. Matthew's throat was feeling dry, and he was starting to get a headache.

"Having said that," Charles continued, "my family is more important to me than the air I breathe, and I would never do anything to hurt Michelle's feelings."

Matthew attempted a half smile. "So you're prepared to tolerate me for Michelle's sake."

"I wouldn't say it that way," Charles said, "but I can't help feeling the way I do about our differences."

"Mr. White," Matthew said, "I think you should know that I didn't want to impose on you today, but Michelle assured me that you were okay with it. But I see you are not really okay. I know it's not easy for you . . . or me."

"No," Charles shook his head, "it's not easy."

Anna's voice came from the patio, calling Charles to come join her. Both men rejoined the party with pasted-on smiles. Charles walked up to the center of the gathering, where Anna was waiting for him, and just as he was about to raise his glass to their closest loved ones, Ben and Michelle appeared carrying a big easel, followed by the diminutive artist who was weighted down by a large frame draped in white silk. He carefully propped it on the easel.

"Surprise!" Ben said to his parents. "Happy anniversary!"

Anna and Charles walked up to the painting and were delighted when the unveiling revealed a beaming image of their two children, lifelike and eternal at the same time.

Matthew leaned against one of the pillars of the patio, encircled by a rainfall of scented honeysuckle, and enjoyed observing Michelle from the background. She looked so lovely and in her element, surrounded by her family. A few minutes passed with cheers from the crowd and many people congratulating the artist, who was floating in the compliments about his work. Three fit and tanned middle-aged men were talking; they could not see Matthew through the wall of vegetation, but he could hear them clearly.

"Isn't that painting a great gift?" said the oldest of the three as they began a conversation.

"So, is that Michelle's young man in the ponytail?" another said nodding toward the people gathered near the painting.

"No, that's the artist who painted the portrait," said the second one. "Michelle's guy is tall with dark hair and is wearing a dark blue jacket."

"Thank goodness that's not him," said the first one. "I can't get used to men in ponytails. So which one is he? Do you see him from here?"

"I'll point him out when I see him." The third friend let out a little laugh. "He's a nice looking young man. no ponytail."

"Well, good," said the first friend. "At least he's got his looks."

"What do you mean?" the second one asked.

"You know how Charles feels about the whole thing," the third friend replied. "He had quite a struggle to bring his business back after the boy almost trashed it. You read the article. Charles would rather eat his toes than admit it, but he dreads the thought that Michelle might eventually marry the boy."

"It's too early in the game to worry about that," number two replied. "You know how young people are. Michelle may be dating that other guy by Christmas."

"You mean Yannik?" the third one asked.

"Naturally," the first friend said. "Look at him right now. He's buzzing around Michelle like a bee to honey. The guy has a brain in his head, getting his PhD any day now, and he helps at the bookshop. What a kind soul."

They all broke out in a deep belly laugh.

That was more than Matthew wanted to hear. At that very moment, a loud clinking of glasses announced the toast. Charles and Anna, addressing the assembled familiar faces, raised their glasses.

"Dear friends," Charles spoke, his voice choking slightly, "I am intensely moved by the love that surrounds me tonight. With Anna, we have been blessed with a strong love and companionship, a fantastic family, the best friends in the world, and, as if anyone could ask for more, God has even given us a comfortable home and a thriving business. Although we've had our trials like everyone else, we managed always to stay together and keep our heads high and our values intact. For without our integrity, all the success in the world would mean nothing."

As Charles paused, he looked up into the crowd and

caught Matthew's eye in the briefest glimpse of recognition, as if the message were directed at him. Maybe he was over-sensitive and the conversation he had overheard had hurt his feelings, or maybe . . .

"So tonight I want to make a toast," Charles continued, "to my darling bride of thirty years, to my beautiful children . . . and to old-fashioned values!"

Among the cheers and raised glasses, Matthew could see Michelle standing on her tiptoes looking for him. She hadn't seen him yet. Ben popped his head out from inside the house behind where Matthew had been standing.

"How're you holding up, man?" Ben raised his eyebrows with a smile.

"I've had more fun at the dentist," Matthew replied.

"I know." Ben rolled his eyes. "Who invented speeches? We need some noise. Watch your feet."

Ben rolled wide open the patio doors, and out boomed a glittering explosion of high-cheering, enormous guitars and wide-brimmed sombreros as the Mariachi band made its way center stage to the rapid-fire tune of their vibrato voices. In the commotion, Matthew slipped quietly out the side garden into the night.

CHAPTER FOUR

"WHAT?" SAID CHARLES WHITE, PARKING THE GOLF CART next to the clubhouse.

His three golf buddies gave him a knowing look and sat down around the table in the terrace in a well-rehearsed routine developed over many years of shared camaraderie. The late summer air brought in the slightest chill, the first hint that the season was turning. A majestic maple tree shading the terrace dropped one single golden leaf as if agreeing with the wind that it was time for a change.

"Come on," said Charles, "you've been acting weird for eighteen holes. Out with it."

"Great party last night," said Clyde, the more outgoing

of the foursome and the minister of the church they all attended.

"Clyde," said Charles, "you've said that about ten times already. It was a good party, except for you-know-who disappearing in the middle of it."

"Not in the middle of it," said Brian, a successful physician and the youngest of the four. "It was actually after your speech that he went missing."

The three men snickered.

"What?" said Charles. "There you go again."

"All right," said Jack, the fourth golf partner, an elegant and reserved art gallery owner. "I'm not one to interfere, but I think he might have taken it as an intentional slight to him. You know, he's a bright guy. He must have known that you had shown the article to everybody you know. Then what you told us that you said to him in your study, and then the toast to rub it in. Can't blame him if he didn't feel welcome."

Charles looked at the other two to evaluate whether they were agreeing with Jack. They nodded. The server came over to take their order, deflecting their attention.

"Maybe it *was* directed at him," Charles said when the server left. "There. I admit it. So what's wrong with that?"

"At the risk of sounding preachy," Clyde said with a smile, "he was a guest in your home, and more particularly, he is dating your daughter."

"He's also a dweeb that almost cost me my business a few

years ago," Charles said sucking his cheeks. "I think I'm entitled to speak my mind in my own home."

"Was Michelle upset?" Clyde asked.

"She was awfully quiet but kept her chin up. Probably didn't want to spoil the party," Charles said, "but I heard her talking to Anna in the kitchen when everybody had left. You guys know I wouldn't do anything to upset my daughter, but I can't undo what's been done either. I didn't choose to have Matthew Swift as a potential son-in-law, and frankly, I won't be losing any sleep if their relationship doesn't work out. There, I said it."

Their sandwiches arrived. As they began to eat, Clyde told a story. The other three friends relaxed and listened, as Clyde was one of those people born with the gift of story-telling. He could hold an audience for hours, remembering names and dates and places and weaving through a tale as if he was reading from a book.

"A colleague of mine was involved in prison ministry," Clyde started. "His name was Henry. Let me just say that my friend Henry weighed about 260 pounds and stood six feet five inches tall—a giant. Not just physically; the man was also a giant spiritually. He was as tall and well built in his heart as he was in frame. To Henry, working in a prison was just like working anywhere else. Whenever I asked him if he had ever feared for his own safety, he would laugh. He wasn't afraid of anyone, not even these mean, ruthless criminals with whom he was sharing the gospel. I was always amazed at the stories of how God would use Henry to communicate with murderers, thieves, and all types of tough criminals. Many of these men would pray to receive Christ, and often Henry would stay in touch with them for years."

Clyde paused to take a bite of his sandwich and assess the interest of the audience. His three friends were locked into listening mode.

"One afternoon," Clyde continued, "I got a call from Henry. He sounded very subdued, almost depressed, very unlike Henry. So I asked him what was wrong. As it happens, that day, on one of his regular visits to the state prison, he was guided to a section he had not visited before. The guards were instructed to let him in and out of the cells upon his request. This was a type of solitary confinement ward; the men kept here were either considered dangerous or were being punished for causing an altercation in the facility. When he called me on the phone, Henry had already been in there for several hours and was taking a break. He was frustrated that the day hadn't been very fruitful, and he asked me to pray for him. I asked him what he thought might be the problem, and he didn't know. He was very confused.

"The first cell he had gone into contained a murderer serving a life sentence. He was a rough character, equal in bulk to Henry's considerable heft, and with the attitude to go with it. Henry said that after thirty minutes of talking, the inmate was praying along with Henry, asking Jesus to come into his heart.

"The second inmate was in for big-time drug dealing. He could be out in four years with good conduct, but he'd been having trouble keeping control of his temper, and that was hurting his chances of rehabilitation. Just like the first inmate, during Henry's visit he had found it in his heart to pray and ask for God's help in finding his way.

"Henry said that after that, all the other inmates he visited just refused to have anything to do with him and rejected him in such a way that it made Henry question his ability to continue with this work. I said to Henry that if the first two visits had gone so well, the key had to be in the third inmate. So I asked him a simple question: What happened in the third cell?"

Clyde paused and looked at Charles for a second or two.

"So who was in the third cell?" Charles asked.

"Henry was finding it hard to tell me," Clyde continued and kept looking at Charles. "I could hear that his voice was tighter, as if on the verge of tears. Henry said that in each of the first two cells he had felt pumped with success, but what he saw in the third cell took him by surprise. There was a transvestite in there. Even with the prison uniform, he had managed to keep his appearance decidedly androgynous. He looked at Henry with sad, miserable eyes. Henry admitted that he had been repulsed and felt sick in the stomach, so he just decided to skip that cell and move on to the next. Then Henry said that from that point on, God had not used him anymore. Not one person seemed to have any interest in the truth that he was sharing. So do you want to know what I said to Henry?"

Clyde again was looking at Charles.

"Why do I have a feeling that you are going to tell me anyway?" Charles said, and the others chuckled.

"Nothing," said Clyde. "I didn't say a word. I just kept saying a silent prayer for Henry and listened to his reaction. After a very long pause, Henry spoke again. Without the need for me to explain what had happened, he knew it with his own heart. I sighed with relief because I knew that Henry was going to be okay. He said that he had now realized, more than ever, that it was not up to him to pick and choose who was worthy of God's grace. Because if he did that, God would be out of business. Because if he had to be honest, the bottom line is that nobody would really qualify. None of us are worthy!"

As Charles heard the end to his friend's story, he knew that the whole story had been directed at him. Bless Clyde. He had done it again. He had the gift of seeing straight into people's hearts. The next day, after a sleepless night and a surprisingly convicting message on a similar topic at church, Charles pulled a Post-it note with a name and phone number from the door of the refrigerator and went straight to the phone. When the voice at the other end picked up, Charles cleared his throat.

"Matthew," he said, "it's Charles White. I have a proposal that I want you to consider."

CHAPTER FIVE

As promised, Michelle was spending her Sunday afternoon helping Matthew set up the new store. She was puzzled at Matthew's smile as he ended his phone conversation and put his cell phone back in his pocket.

"That was your dad," Matthew said.

"My dad called *you*?" Michelle asked, arching her eyebrows.

"Yep," Matthew replied, digging back into a stack of catalogues he had started sorting before his phone rang. "He had a proposal. He offered to share with me some information that might help me with my business. He said we'd keep it light, and we could get together for half an hour, maybe four or five times. That's all."

Michelle considered the proposal in silence as they both kept working through the stacks of supplies. The store needed a lot of work still, and there had been a few glitches. The walls had been painted a pale eggshell color over the much darker blue from the previous tenant, and when it dried it was evident that the base coat had not managed to cover the blue, resulting in a blend of streaks in an alarming shade of moldy cream cheese. The paint job would have to be redone, meaning that they would be hard-pressed to finish setting up before opening. On the upside, the signs had just been finished, and the ample shop front looked really smart and modern.

"So . . . did you agree?" Michelle asked, keeping her tone casual.

Matthew shrugged. "I figured it couldn't get any worse with your dad."

"You're probably right," Michelle said and laughed.

"It must not have been easy for him to pick up the phone and call me," said Matthew, "so I have to respect that."

"And of course what you are not saying is that you are doing it for me," Michelle said, batting her eyelashes.

"You're worth it." Matthew winked back.

Michelle had an unaffected natural laugh that cheered up everyone around her. Beyond the humor, however, there was a great deal of truth in what Michelle had just said. After the fiasco at the anniversary party, Matthew had thrown himself into his work, as he usually did whenever his emotions over-crowded his thoughts. He had to admit to himself that he had felt unduly judged and rejected at the party, and he was still shaken. Every bone in his body ached to please Michelle, and knowing how much family meant to her, the incident had left him insecure and exposed, aware that if he couldn't find a way to fit into her family, there would always be a cloud over their relationship. He had accepted Charles's invitation on this basis, not because he expected to learn anything from her father, an almost-retired sports merchandise business owner, but because he hoped it would bridge the gap between them.

"So when is the first meeting?" Michelle asked.

"Tomorrow, after work," Matthew said, "in your bookstore."

"Really?" Michelle laughed again.

"What do you think?" Matthew asked. "Your dad sug-gested it, so he must have thought of it as neutral ground."

"Sounds like a good idea," Michelle said. "I'll make sure to hide any sharp objects."

There was a knock on the front glass door, which startled them, as they didn't expect anybody to show up on a Sunday afternoon. Matthew recognized the owner of the building, his landlord, and walked to the door to let him in. From the back of the store Michelle could see the two men having a long con-versation. Matthew held the door open, but the landlord remained standing outside. From the body language and the gestures, it didn't look like good news. She went into the back room and started to unpack the electric water heater and the mugs she had brought as a present for Matthew, along with a package of herbal teas. After what seemed to Michelle like a long half hour, the landlord left, and Matthew locked the door again with a deliberate slam. He slunk back to the office and slumped down on the floor, with his head in his hands. Michelle handed him a cup of hot tea and waited. It took a few minutes before Matthew could speak.

"I don't believe this guy," he said shaking his head. "He just stopped by to casually say that there's a problem with the lease."

"What problem?" Michelle asked softly as she sat next to him on the floor. She had never seen Matthew in this mood. He had been full of energy a few minutes ago, but suddenly he looked like someone coming down with the flu.

"A big one," Matthew said. "I don't know if we'll be able to open."

In between sips of tea and frequent head shaking, Matthew told Michelle why the landlord had come to see him. It appeared that the landlord had failed to mention the fact that he was in the middle of divorce proceedings when they signed the lease. His wife's attorney was advising her to sell the building instead of renting it, and the lease that Matthew held, without her consent or signature, was null and void for all legal purposes. The landlord said that he had not approached Matthew sooner because he had been certain that his wife would come around and sign the lease, but the property was now effectively locked in a battle of wills between the two parties. The divorce settlement would free up the property one way or another, but it would take time, and Matthew had already overextended his expenses getting the new store ready and advertising it. He needed to open on schedule or he might have to give up the whole project, taking a huge hit and hurting the original store that was anchoring his expansion plans.

"Wow," Michelle said.

Matthew nodded. "Wow is right."

"It's his fault. If he had told you before you signed, you could have found another location, right?" Michelle asked.

"There isn't another location like this," Matthew said. "The vehicle access is perfect, the anchor store draws lots of traffic, and the visibility from the road is unbeatable. I have to admit that I put some pressure on the guy."

"You did?" she asked.

"Yes," Matthew chewed on the words, "he said he'd get back to me in a few days, and I offered him a higher rent price if he signed the lease then and there. I never in my wildest dreams imagined that the guy didn't actually have the authority to commit to the lease . . . or I would never have pressured him."

Michelle held Matthew's hand for a long time.

"I guess there's no point in continuing today," Matthew said. "Might as well go home."

They both turned off the lights and locked up in silence.

"I'm sure there's a way to sort out the lease problem," Michelle said. "I know you'll find it."

"Thanks, babe," Matthew said. "Thanks for your help today. I'm sorry it was all for nothing. I think I'll call your dad to let him know that there is no need to meet tomorrow."

"Why?"

"Well," Matthew shrugged, "there's no point in mentoring me to open a business that doesn't exist."

"You're not giving up, are you?" Michelle teased. "Maybe you should keep the appointment. Maybe my dad can actually help."

"How?" Matthew asked with a half smile.

"I don't know," Michelle said, "just a gut feeling."

CHAPTER SIX

MATTHEW ARRIVED AT THE BOOKSTORE FIFTEEN MINUTES ahead of his meeting with Charles. He was still reeling from the bombshell that his landlord dropped about the lease and kept running alternative scenarios in his mind that always resulted in the same dead end. If he were to start his new store at all, it would have to be in the location he had leased. The preparations and investment had gone too far to be changed now.

Matthew looked around for Michelle, but there was only Yannik to greet him.

"Matthew!" Yannik called out. "Come in. Michelle just stepped out for a second. She said you can use the office for your meeting, or you can sit in the reading loft if you prefer. It should be pretty quiet today."

"The loft is fine, thanks," Matthew said. "Let Michelle's dad know I'll be upstairs when he arrives."

Matthew preferred to keep the meeting brief, and since the upstairs loft was less formal, he thought that setting was better than an office. It was an open area that could seat about twenty people, and Michelle had arranged it with a cozy smattering of small armchairs and reading lamps that she supplemented with folding chairs for book signings and lectures. Matthew picked up a newspaper from a side table and started reading. Another ghastly article from the "Yours Truly" Brian Brighton character; this time his article was a vendetta hounding a poor restaurant owner who had dared to question the knowledge of the newspaper's food critic. Matthew dismissed the article halfway and flipped through the paper. He heard Charles's voice downstairs and set the paper down.

"Matthew!" Charles said, extending his hand. "It's good to see you. Michelle told me about the awful mess with the landlord. How are you holding up?"

"I've been better," Matthew said, settling back in his chair.

"Let me know if I can help you with anything," Charles said, "anything at all."

"Thank you, Mr. White," Matthew said, "I appreciate it."

"Please, call me Charles," he said.

"Not to sound too gloomy, Charles," Matthew said, "but it seems that I don't have much of a business at the moment, so I don't want to take up your time for nothing. I wouldn't want you to waste your time or for you to be frustrated with me."

Matthew gave Charles some more details about the fateful lease contract as Charles settled in a leather chair diagonally across from him. Charles reflected for a few moments gathering his thoughts. He leaned forward in his chair.

"Matthew," Charles said, "you and I both know that I'm not proud of my conduct at the party the other day, and I have apologized already, so I won't dwell on it any longer."

Charles paused as Matthew waved a dismissive hand, a spontaneous gesture to indicate that whatever was in the past had been forgiven and forgotten.

"But I want to make it clear to you that my offer to mentor you is not a way to ingratiate myself. In fact, it was during a conversation with my golf buddies, Clyde in particular, that the idea came to me. Did you meet Clyde at the party?"

"I'm not sure; I was introduced to a lot of people," Matthew said.

"You would remember Clyde," Charles said. "Anyway, you'll have plenty of opportunities to meet him."

Matthew was taken by surprise by the swell of emotion that filled his heart with Charles's casual way of including him as part of the family in the future. Just a few kind words could generate such a strong response.

"Anyhow," Charles said, "I'm very glad you accepted the

mentoring idea and that you think that an old sock like me can still teach you a trick or two. Actually, I want to share four things with you. It's what I call the 'Four Truths.' When I was going through some rough spots of my own, Clyde taught these truths to me. He's the pastor at our church, a life-time friend of mine, and a former business owner himself. As a Christian, I have always read the Bible, but it wasn't until Clyde helped me understand these particular truths that I began to really apply it to my daily life. Wait a minute. I just realized something . . ."

Charles let out a good chuckle, and Matthew waited for him to continue.

"I just realized," Charles said, "we are sitting in Michelle's bookstore surrounded by hundreds of Bibles in every shape and form; we couldn't have met in a better place!"

"The Truth is all around us," Matthew said.

They shared a hearty laugh.

"Assuming that you're familiar with the Bible," Charles said.

"I am," Matthew said. "In fact, that's how I met Michelle."

"Really?" Charles said with surprise.

"Yes," Matthew said. "I was raised a Christian and attended church regularly all my life, but after the death of my parents, I became disconnected. I still was going through the motions, but I didn't really have a relationship with Christ. It was more like visiting His house but not accepting His hospitality."

"I'm sorry about your parents, Matthew. How old were you when it happened?"

"My father died when I was sixteen. He suffered a long decline with lung cancer, and he hadn't smoked a cigarette in his life. Talk about irony," Matthew said with a slight edge in his voice.

"That must have been so hard for you and your mother," Charles said.

"It was," Matthew said, clearing his throat. "I don't think she ever recovered. I started working and taking over my father's role. I guess I wanted to pretend that nothing bad had happened and that we could do just fine without him. If I'm honest, I was trying to prove to God that I could do fine without Him as well. After my father died we had some financial difficulties. My mother withdrew into herself, and her health became very frail. Her heart gave out three years later. I guess you could say she died of a broken heart. I could not understand why God would take both my parents, two of the most gentle, kind people you'd ever know. Without ever making a conscious decision about it, I shut out God from my life. I couldn't understand His plan for me, couldn't accept that He could love me and still take my parents away. I wanted to be super-human. I couldn't bear anybody feeling sorry for me. I wouldn't let anybody see my pain."

Charles nodded. "It seems to me that your experience wasn't unique. Many Christians I know tend to judge God based on their circumstances."

"Exactly. I was centered on myself. The pursuit of business success became my sole focus; I had become the proverbial carrot chaser, as I've heard you liked to call me." Charles gave an embarrassed grin as Matthew continued. "Then came my spectacular and well-documented fall. It forced me to take a hard look at myself and my priorities. One day I was driving along this street and noticed the Christian bookstore. I still don't know why, but I parked the car and came inside. I asked Michelle what she would recommend for a fallen angel trying to find his way back home, and she handed me a Bible. She said I couldn't go wrong with that book. I kept coming week after week; I think I started the largest private collection of Bibles in three states. So here I am."

"That's wonderful," Charles said.

"I read the Bible that Michelle recommended. It was written in plain English, and, just like you said, I noticed for the first time things that I had read many times before but had never really paid attention to. I gave my life up to Christ, and my life has been filled with so many blessings, the loveliest one being Michelle, of course."

"That's music to a father's ears," Charles said, smiling.

"It's true," Matthew said. "From that moment on I have tried to live for God, without letting pride and ego control my life as before. The only problem is that people still judge me by the way I was before. Sometimes I feel like I'm stuck in a stereotype, and I don't get a chance to prove myself. All I ask for is for people to give me a chance."

Well, here's your chance, kid, Charles thought. *With your natural talent and brains, if you learn how to serve God, there'll be great things in store for you.* Charles couldn't even believe he was having these thoughts, knowing he had once been the kid's worst judge.

"Matthew, that was a wonderful decision you made. And let me tell you that I am proud of you. You have taken a big step of faith. And God does forgive you. God also wants you to live for Him. But there's an enemy. Do you know who God's enemy is?"

"The IRS?" Matthew said.

Charles grinned.

"Of course," Charles said, "but seriously, you need to know that there are forces that you can call evil if you prefer, but I call him by his first name, Satan. Whatever you want to call him, he is active today trying to deceive people like you and me and keep us from doing what God wants us to do."

Matthew hesitated. "To be honest, I am not sure I really understand the whole Satan thing."

"It's important that you're aware that Satan doesn't want you to have a fresh start. Satan is not happy about this decision you've made to become a Christian. Since he was not successful in preventing it, he'll be working in different ways."

"How do you mean?" Matthew asked in a curious voice.

"He'll try to get in the way. He'll interfere. He'll try to get you to go back to your same old rut and to make you feel like God has no real value impact in your life. You see, when

Satan fails at preventing someone from becoming a Christian, his goal changes. His new goal is to keep that person from living like a Christian."

"You sound so sure," Matthew said softly.

Charles shrugged. "Because it happened to me," he said. "That's how I know. That's why I would like to share the Four Truths with you, because they were a big help for me and still are. Staying focused on God is a constant battle." Charles leaned forward in his seat. "So if you're ready, I'd like to share the first truth with you."

"Shoot," Matthew said.

"Let's see. First let me give you a little background for context. The reason we call these the Four Truths is because Clyde reminded me that there are good truths or principles in the Bible that can help anyone in life and business. Basically, he taught me four of them to focus on that could help me live out my faith at home and at work. The first truth, for example, is something that I had heard many times before but had never really understood. It was a few years ago that I finally got it, when my business was almost knocked out of the game; you remember, right? In a way you could say you played a part in my enlightenment."

"Hey," Matthew said, "I won't take credit for that."

They both laughed, and any remaining tension in the room disappeared.

"At that time everything felt so dark to me. I couldn't enjoy my family, I certainly didn't enjoy my job, I even stopped playing golf and meeting my friends. For the first time in my life, I didn't feel like going to work in the morning. The great company I had built was failing. We were going under. Facing the collapse of my world, and blaming myself for my failure, for the first time I said a different kind of prayer. I gave it all up."

Charles stopped and stretched his legs out. He stroked the leather armrests and looked down at his feet, as if trying to find the right words.

"I didn't give up in the traditional sense. What I mean is that I handed the wheel over to God. I gave up my pride and my obstinacy, and for the first time I said, 'God, if it is Your will for my business to close, then let it be so. Show me Your way, and I will follow.'"

Matthew rubbed the bridge of his nose.

"Am I losing you?" Charles asked.

"Not at all," Matthew said. "It's just that I haven't slept much lately."

"I know what you mean," Charles nodded. "I've been there."

"Please continue," Matthew said.

"Truth Number One," Charles said, "as my friend Clyde would put it, is: We must choose to follow God's agenda instead of our own. To make it personal, Matthew, you must decide if you are going to follow God's agenda or your own."

Charles stretched his back as if getting ready to get up. Matthew pressed on.

"So?" Matthew asked. "Did you get an answer to your

TRUTH #1
We must choose
God's agenda instead of our own.

prayer?"

"Boy, did I get an answer!" Charles said. "You see, until then, every time that I had prayed for God's will, what I really meant was that I would follow His plan as long as it met with my approval first. I had never really surrendered entirely to His agenda. If you had asked me at the time, I would have told you that nobody knows what's best for me better than myself. Now I know that God has a very specific plan and purpose for me. I constantly pray and seek that plan. I have to stay focused on Him. Every time I get carried away and start focusing on myself, I get off track. As a business-man, I had a tendency to set goals and allow the pursuit of those goals to consume me. I now recognize that those goals were really more my goals than God's plan. I still set goals today, and I work hard to achieve them, but I keep an open mind, always looking to see where God is working. I don't hesitate to put God first. Satan dangles carrots out there for us to chase. He tries to get us off the path God has for us. Quite frankly, he doesn't care how close we are to the path God has for us, as long as we are not on it."

"Then how do you know when you are really on God's

plan and not chasing Satan's carrot?" Matthew asked.

"That's a great question, and the answer is to get to know God more. The more time I spend reading the Bible and praying to God, the more alert I am to Satan's carrots. It is the truth that will set you free. You have often heard that jewelry experts recognize the fake stones not by studying fakes but by studying the real ones. It was like that for me. At first I didn't recognize the shape that the answers to my prayers were coming in. People would talk to me and share their advice, my wife, my friend Clyde, and even my bank called to say that they had reconsidered a bank loan that they had turned down, all these people so full of wisdom that I was able to see now that I had taken Satan's blinders off. I was just trying too hard, and God had been trying to help me all the time. You know the rest of the story: the business survived and is now stronger than before because we are better prepared for the ups and downs. In your case, you could take your problem with your landlord as an example."

Matthew blinked rapidly as if trying to focus.

"What about it?" he asked.

"Well," Charles continued, "your landlord seems to be going through a rough time."

"A divorce," Matthew replied, "which he didn't mention until this Sunday, so I had no idea when I signed the lease."

"Why do you think he did that?" Charles asked.

"He didn't want to lose the deal," Matthew said. He paused for a moment. "I have to admit that I put some pressure on him."

"That's what I mean," Charles interrupted. "There may be something there. Maybe God is more interested in how you deal with the landlord than in whether the lease is valid or not."

Charles slapped his knees and pulled himself to his feet. Matthew followed and they both started walking toward the stairs. Charles rested his hand briefly on Matthew's shoulder.

"God has a great plan for your life, Matthew," he said.

At that moment Michelle popped her head out at the bottom of the stairs. She waited until they had reached the bottom and handed Matthew and Charles a lollipop each.

"There you are!" Michelle said. "For bravery."

"It didn't hurt too much, I hope," Charles laughed and looked up at Matthew.

"Didn't hurt at all," Matthew said, popping the candy in his mouth.

CHAPTER SEVEN

MATTHEW WAITED FOR THE LIGHT TO CHANGE. INSTEAD of turning into the parking lot of the new store today, he was driving just three intersections further to meet with the landlord about the controversy over the validity of the lease. As he drove past the store—his perfect location, his shattered dream—he couldn't help but mentally blast the landlord and his wife and the whole convoluted reason for pulling out of the rental agreement. He, of course, had the option to sue, in which case his claim was likely to get tied into the divorce proceedings and add insult to injury. He could also put pressure on the landlord, but that would not really be any match to the pressure already being put on by the landlord's wife.

Matthew's mind wandered as the light for the opposite lane turned from red to green, then to red again. Charles's words were still ringing in his ears. *Choose God's agenda.* But how would he know the difference between God's agenda and his own? How could he tell if his plans were simply a reflection of what God had intended for him, or if he was just pushing his own ambitions and chasing the proverbial carrot? How could he tell the difference?

Matthew parked and rang the bell at his landlord's office. Mr. Velez promptly came to the door and shook Matthew's hand, barely making eye contact.

"Matthew," said Mr. Velez, "come in."

Matthew looked around the sparsely decorated office. Every object was there for a purpose—the desk, the filing cabinets, and the document sorter on the wall. The only item present not for utility but for decoration was a gilded portrait frame with a wedding photo of a very young Mr. Velez and a striking olive-skinned beauty with tiny white flowers woven into her glossy black hair. The bride and groom were smiling into the camera, with eyes full of the future, and hands intertwined. How do people start from there and get to an ugly divorce throwing threats and insults across a lawyer's conference table? Mr. Velez caught Matthew's eye.

"That's our problem," he said. "Right there—Mrs. Velez."

Matthew couldn't find anything to say.

"We were so in love," Mr. Velez continued. "We couldn't

bear to stay a minute away from each other. Now we can barely spend a minute in the same room without combusting into a screaming argument. Anyway, you are not here to talk about my troubles."

Something in the way Mr. Velez said those words gave Matthew a start, as if he had been napping on a bus and a fellow passenger had given him a soft nudge. No, he wasn't here to talk about Mr. Velez's divorce and his personal problems. He was here to talk about his business and the aggravation and expenses that Mrs. Velez's intransigent position had brought upon him. Yet now that he had seen the photograph, and the sorrow in Mr. Velez's eyes, somehow he didn't feel like talking about anything at all.

"Mr. Velez . . ." Matthew started, but couldn't continue.

"Matthew," Mr. Velez said, "I wish I could have better news for you, but my wife is not budging. She is intent on going ahead with her own plan, and she insists that the rental agreement is null and void. Technically she is right, as we know, but I was hoping that she could see the merits of renting the property to you since the lease, in the event she still wanted to sell it, would only add value to the property. But she would not consider it, probably just to punish me in some way, and this seems to be her final word. I am so sorry."

Matthew nodded slowly. Both men stood in awkward silence, unsure of what should follow.

"I understand if you initiate legal action," Mr. Velez said, looking away through the window. "I would, of course, pre-fer if we could find an amicable way to sort this out."

"Mr. Velez," Matthew said, "you know that I have already incurred several expenses related to the opening; I had started to set up the place, and . . ."

Matthew couldn't muster up any of the indignation that he had felt in the car. He couldn't even remember the long list of grievances he had planned to spurt out to his landlord. Instead, all he could think of was the difference in the eyes of the man looking at him right now and the young man in the wedding photograph. He decided he needed to make up a reason to escape from the office right then.

"Listen, Mr. Velez," Matthew said, looking at the clock on the wall, "I apologize, but I forgot that I was supposed to pick up my girlfriend fifteen minutes ago. I really have to run. Let me come back in about an hour, and we can continue this conversation."

"No problem." Mr. Velez seemed as relieved as Matthew to put an end to the uncomfortable meeting.

Matthew got in his car with a lump in his throat. He did not understand what had just happened. He was not one to shy away from conflict; he had always dealt with situations immediately and decisively. Yet now he felt he needed to talk to someone to sort out the best decision, and the person to talk to was Michelle. He drove up to her bookstore and found her upstairs on her knees arranging an area rug decorated with a brightly colored alphabet.

"It's for kiddy's story time tomorrow," Michelle said, shrugging her shoulders and grinning. "It's a new idea. What do you think?"

"Lovely, like everything you do," Matthew said. "Can I talk to you for a second? I need your opinion on something."

Michelle sat cross-legged on the carpet.

"I just went to see the landlord about the lease," Matthew said.

"So did his wife come around?"

"Not a chance," he said. "She's digging her heels in. He's pretty gutted about it."

"Oh, no!" Michelle said. "That's terrible. I really thought she might agree in the end."

"I think it's the divorce," Matthew said. "It makes you do things that you would never do to a person you love."

"So what did you say to him?" she asked.

"Well," Matthew said, "that's the thing. I didn't know what to say."

"Really?" Michelle asked. "Doesn't sound like you!"

"Exactly," he said. "On the drive to his office I was stewing over all this list of expenses that I've incurred and commitments that I had taken up based on the lease of the store. Then when we were face-to-face, there was something in the way he looked at me, or rather in the way he *couldn't* look at me . . . and the wedding photograph."

"What wedding photograph?" she asked.

Matthew described Mr. Velez's photograph and how he

couldn't bring himself to build up a confrontation or threaten to sue the landlord.

"I bet I'm going to regret this," Matthew said, "but I think I'm not going to sue him. I had this strange feeling in there. He was trying to talk to me about what he was going through with his life. He was in pain. I couldn't help but think that in a small way I contributed to the situation by putting pressure on him to sign the lease. Of course, I had no idea that his wife was going to divorce him, but still I feel a little bit responsible. When we were negotiating the lease, I pushed him to sign, saying that I had another location in mind and that I had to know right away. It's not really ethical, but not unusual in business. It's just the cards you play to get what you want. But I'm guessing that part of his omission to have his wife sign the lease was due to my rushing him to sign then and there. Now I am really torn. I feel like apologizing to the man and slapping him at the same time. What do you think? This is no way to do business, I know. I'm totally confused. I think that I would really like to reach out to Mr. Velez, make him feel better if I can. Have I lost it?"

Michelle looked up at him and paused. She got up and slipped her arms around his waist.

"Oh, honey," she said, pulling him tight toward her, "that is the most beautiful thing I have ever heard you say. Of course you haven't lost it. You've never been so on target. I am so proud of you!"

Matthew kissed the top of her head and then held her arms out so that he could look into her eyes.

"So you don't think I've gone mad?"

"Quite the contrary," Michelle said. "I think you've come to your senses."

With renewed conviction, Matthew drove back to the landlord's office. As he was driving past the new store, he noticed a small group of people in dark clothes gathered around the entrance. He drove on to find a place to turn around, and as fast as he could he pulled into the store. As he approached the front door, he noticed the other vehicle parked there—a police cruiser.

CHAPTER EIGHT

"THE POLICE WERE AT THE NEW STORE?" CHARLES SAID arching his thick eyebrows. "Whatever for?"

Charles was seated in the same leather chair upstairs in Michelle's bookstore, and Matthew had settled into the chair he had used before, as if they had choreographed a routine to ease them back into conversation. The only difference today was the brightly colored alphabet rug under their feet. Matthew was retelling the events of the previous day.

"It was just a courtesy visit," Matthew smirked, "to let me know that Mrs. Velez, the landlord's wife, would have a trespassing order issued against me if I didn't vacate the premises in ten days."

"Amazing," Charles said, "but not surprising. People act out of character when they are under such emotionally charged situations as a divorce. So have you decided what you are going to do?"

"Yes," Matthew said. "I had made the decision before I met the police. In fact, I was so surprised about my own reaction that I had to ask Michelle if I was losing my mind."

"And what was the verdict from my daughter?" Charles said with a chuckle.

"Actually, she said something quite peculiar," Matthew said. "She said that on the contrary, I had come to my senses!"

"In those words?" Charles almost jumped out of his seat.

Matthew nodded.

"What was she referring to exactly?" Charles asked. "I find this very interesting."

Matthew related the events of the previous day, including his visit to the landlord and his conversation with Michelle, while Charles smiled to himself, amused.

"If you don't mind," Charles asked, "what was the decision?"

"Well," Matthew said, "when I stopped for my little chat with the police, I was on my way to see the landlord, so I drove over to his office. I told him that I would not pursue any legal action, and I apologized for putting pressure on him to sign."

"Was he surprised?"

"You should have seen his eyes," Matthew said. "It was

like offering water to a man lost in the desert. He hugged me, and hugged me again, and then couldn't help it and started to cry. He had so much on his mind, and the separation from his wife was tearing him into pieces. Mr. Velez said that he felt as if now that what was most important to him had been broken, everything else was coming down with it. And you know what? He offered his moving van and two men to help me move the materials out."

"That's decent of him," Charles said.

"Yep," Matthew said. "He also said he would try to help me find another location to rent, although I doubt that he'll have any success. I had been looking for six months before I found his place."

"So tell me, Matthew," Charles asked, "what made you change your mind and come to that decision then?"

"I can't explain it," Matthew said. "All I can say is that I was on my way to see the landlord the first time, my blood boiling and thinking of all the things I would say to him, and then suddenly I didn't feel like that anymore. It was almost physical, this thing, as if somebody had nudged me from the inside."

Charles slapped the armrests of the leather chair.

"That is truly fantastic," Charles said. "It sounds like you already experienced Truth Number Two. You're way ahead of me!"

"How do you mean?"

"Do you know the story of the prodigal son from the Bible?"

"I'm not sure," Matthew said.

"It's from Luke 15:11–32," Charles said. "The younger son of a wealthy man gathered all he had and left for a far-away land where he squandered everything. He ended up hiring himself off as a laborer. One day, he was feeding the pigs for his employer and found himself so hungry that he started to crave the pigs' food. That's when he came to his senses. He realized that he had everything back home, and he had been misled by Satan to throw it all away. He decided to go back to his father and ask for forgiveness."

"Did it work out in the end?" Matthew asked.

"Yes," Charles said, "the older son protested when his father welcomed the prodigal son back and fed and clothed him. But the father simply said that they should be glad, because the lost son was dead and now he had come back and was alive again."

"So you are saying that I had the same type of moment as the prodigal son in the pigpen, even though in my case I was not experiencing anything near a lack of food and shelter?"

"I think so," Charles said. "You had what I call a 'come to your senses' moment, and that is Truth Number Two: We must recognize the carrots."

TRUTH #2
We must recognize the carrots.

"Still don't see it," Matthew said.

"Let me tell you what happened to me," Charles said. "This was some years back, when Michelle was little and Ben was still a toddler. Anna needed me more than any other time as she dealt with keeping the home and raising two kids. My reaction at the time was to work like a maniac. I thought that the more I worked, the better I could provide for my family, so that was my focus. I was putting in long days, sometimes working weekends as well, basically burning the candle at both ends. I couldn't understand why my wife was unhappy, or why little Michelle kept clinging to me and didn't want to go to work in the mornings. The whole atmosphere at home was stressful. I did a lot of praying. One day I decided to hire another employee to delegate part of my workload. It worked beautifully. My office started running like clockwork, and I was able to get home at five thirty every day. My wife was happy, and the kids were thriving. It was beautiful."

"So that was your pigpen moment?" Matthew said. "Hiring more help?"

"Not at all," Charles said. "While everything was settling nicely, I was able to focus on the important decisions; and as a consequence, business was on the rise and new customers were calling from all over the place. One particular customer wanted us to open a distribution center just outside of Houston. I was pumped. Everything was coming together. I imagine it must feel like that for an actor to see his name in neon lights for the first time."

"That's fantastic," Matthew said. "It's what I'm aiming for."

"Well, I thought so too," Charles said. He ran his hand through his hair and rolled his eyes.

"I'm getting a feeling that it wasn't as good as it sounds," Matthew said.

"At the time it sounded really good," Charles continued. "The margins were going to be incredibly tight, but the volume was unbelievable. We were going to tie down the East Coast, West Coast, and the Caribbean in one swing. Even the bank jumped on the wave and approved a huge increase to our line of credit. You wouldn't believe how quickly everything lined up."

"But since you are not operating in Texas right now, something must have happened," Matthew said.

"As you can imagine, every evening when I got home it was all I could talk about. Anna could hardly get a word in sideways. The Houston project dominated my life. One evening I got home when Anna had just managed to soothe Ben to sleep after he had been fussy with a cold all day. She was exhausted and hoping for some help, and all I could do was sit at the kitchen table and babble on about Houston. To top it off, I was talking too loud and woke up Ben. Just then, little Michelle wanted me to read her a bedtime story, and I said I was too tired. That was the last straw. Anna sat me down and let me know exactly how she felt."

"Uh-oh," Matthew said, "she wasn't happy."

"Naturally," Charles said. "I didn't see it at the time, but all she could look forward to once Houston opened was for me to be away for days at a time and possibly even some weekends. My reaction was to tell her that she didn't appreciate how important this opportunity was for us because she didn't know anything about business. I was patronizing and quite obnoxious, and I walked right out the front door."

"I'm still trying to follow how this relates to the pigpen," Matthew remarked.

"That's when I had my first 'come to your senses' moment," Charles said. "I walked out of that door with my head on fire. I was so upset and irritated. I walked around the block in circles without even noticing what I was doing. Then it happened. One step I was seething, and the next I saw it so clearly. I had been praying so hard for God to ease my workload, and He had answered my prayers by sending me an excellent employee to help me. Then when the Houston opportunity arrived, I had assumed that it came from God as well. I had been wrong. Now I could see plain as day that this new development was a carrot that Satan was dangling in front of me trying to get me to compromise my family time and to steal the blessing that God had so graciously provided. I had taken the bait and had jumped in headfirst."

"So that is what you mean by the pigpen?"

"The pigpen in our lives can be any place where God does not intend for us to be, any situation that falls short of God's plan for us. It's Satan who wants us to stay in the pigpen. Just look around at people you know who supposedly have everything—money, health, a family—and they still are miserable. The key to coming to your senses is to realize that when you are in the pigpen, it is really Satan who is trying to trap you into making a commitment that will keep you stuck there. Once you see this, you have a choice to return to God. That is exactly what I did; I ran back home and hugged my wife. I didn't have to say anything to Anna because she read it in my eyes. I decided not to go to Houston, and as it turned out, my company had the best year ever. I'll never know for sure, but I have a suspicion that the Texas deal would have stretched us too thin. So there you go; that's the story."

"So what you are saying is that maybe I have been looking at what's happening with the store in the wrong way, that maybe there's a blessing in disguise somewhere?" Matthew asked.

"That is beyond our ability to know," Charles said. "We can't always find the answer to all the 'what ifs' of life, but I do believe that we know, deep inside, when we are in the pigpen, and all we need to do is lift up our heads to find the answer. It seems to me that this is exactly what you did yesterday."

"Nobody has ever said anything like that to me before," Matthew said. "Thank you, Charles, I really appreciate it."

"You know, Matthew," he said, getting up from the chair and stretching his back, "when we started this, I wasn't sure that you were ready to listen."

"And now?" Matthew said.

"You're catching up," Charles said, laughing.

As they both started walking back downstairs, Matthew began thinking that he would pay more attention in the future to not get trapped in the pigpen again. What he didn't know was how soon he would be testing this truth.

CHAPTER NINE

TRUE TO HIS WORD, MR. VELEZ ARRANGED FOR A TRUCK
and two men to help Matthew move the boxes and display
bed frames back into the storage area of the main store.
The truck would be coming at the crack of dawn the next
day, so Matthew made his best attempt to check that everything was packed and ready to go. He moved quickly and
forced himself not to think about what might have been,
going over a final inspection before he handed over the
keys to the landlord. Alone, in the emptiness of the store,
Matthew felt a pang of regret for letting the landlord and
his wife get off so easily from their commitment. What a
pointless waste of energy and money this whole idea had

been. To make it worse, the staff at the main store was avoiding the subject, obviously trying not to embarrass him, which of course irritated Matthew even more. His cell rang.

"Is this Matthew Swift?" asked the nasal voice of the caller. "This is Brian Brighton from the *Morning Standard*."

Matthew didn't reply. The voice continued.

"I'm the guy from the Yours Truly column," he said. "I don't know if you read my piece about you recently. I'm doing a follow-up on your story."

"This isn't really a good time," Matthew said.

"It'll just take a moment," Brighton said. "I just wanted to give you the opportunity to make a statement, you know, give you a fair chance."

"To be honest," Matthew said, "I don't care for your column at all."

"I can imagine," Brighton said. "I don't care much for it myself, but it pays the mortgage, you know. Good news doesn't sell."

"Well," Matthew said, "I'm afraid I have no comment for you."

"I understand," Brighton said, "but I think it is only fair to warn you that I am running the story of the failed expansion and the voided lease. I spoke with Mrs. Velez already. Your landlord's wife."

"I'm aware of who Mrs. Velez is," Matthew said.

There was silence on the other side.

"What did she say?" Matthew finally asked.

"Nothing," Brighton said. "She wouldn't make any comment. Off the record she said that she felt sorry that you had gotten caught up in the middle of her divorce."

"So who told you about the lease then?" Matthew asked.

"He wants to remain anonymous, and I have to protect my sources," Brighton said. "All I can say is that he overheard your conversation with another guy. Apparently you were talking in a bookstore. Walls have ears; you should be more careful, you know."

"Thanks for your concern," Matthew said. "I'm touched."

"You can be sarcastic," Brighton said. "I'm used to it. It's my job to keep my nose in everything."

"Your job is disgusting," Matthew said. "You feed on other people's misery."

"I don't create the misery," he said. "Most of the time they bring it upon themselves."

"Is that what you tell yourself so you can sleep at night?" Matthew asked.

"It's the truth. A lot of people drown in a glass of water. What's a problem to one is an opportunity to another. Like the Seven Seas store, you know? They're trying to get out of their lease and are stuck, and on the other hand you are trying to get a lease and can't find a location. It's ironic, and it makes for a good story. Makes my job easy. Failure stories almost write themselves."

"Good for you," Matthew said. "Excuse me, but I have to

finish clearing out the failure that you'll be writing about, so I have to go now."

Matthew turned off his cell phone, locked up leaving his packing and inventory undone, and drove off to meet Michelle at their usual coffee shop for breakfast. She was waiting for him at their table by the window, sipping her coffee and reading the newspaper.

"Hey, babe!" She squinted as the sun hit her eyes. "I was reading the column by that guy, Yours Truly. He's talking about a poor man who lost his shirt trying to open an all-organic restaurant."

"Coincidence. He just called me on my cell phone," Matthew said, settling in with his coffee.

"The organic restaurant guy?" she asked.

"No," Matthew said, "Brian Brighton, the journalist."

"What did he want?"

"Blood," Matthew said. "He has the scoop about my latest misadventure."

"Oh, no!" Michelle cried.

"Apparently somebody overheard my conversation with your dad in the bookstore the other day, and that somebody called Brighton and gave him the full details, so he's writing a follow-up story on me."

"Can he do that?" Michelle asked.

"Apparently."

They both drank their coffee in silence, staring at the folded newspaper as if it were a coiled rattlesnake.

"Can't you do something about it?" Michelle inquired. "Do you want me to talk to Dad?"

"No, thanks," he replied curtly. "You've done enough already."

"What do you mean?" Michelle said.

"I mean that it was your idea for me to talk to your dad," he said, "and if I hadn't had that conversation, then Brighton would not have heard about it."

"No it wasn't; that's not fair," Michelle said. "Dad is only trying to help. Just yesterday he said how much he admired you for not suing the landlord."

"Yes, well," Matthew rolled his eyes, "for all the good that did to my bank balance."

"It's not all about the money, is it?" she asked.

"No, of course it isn't. It's about my pride and my reputation with my employees, and about whoever it was who overheard the conversation and ratted off to Brighton."

"I don't understand," Michelle said.

"Of course you do," Matthew argued. "You just don't want to admit it. It was your precious friend Yannik!"

"Impossible!" she said.

"Of course it was him," Matthew snapped. "Who else? He was there at the bookstore all the time, and he knew about the first article that Brighton wrote about me. He hates my guts and wants to clear the way to get to you."

"That's not right." Michelle's eyes filled with tears. "You don't know for sure that it was him."

"Go on, protect him," Matthew said and stood up so fast that he almost fell backward. "It's always like that. 'Yannik is perfect, he is such a humanitarian.' I'm the heartless vulture who only cares about the business. I've heard it before, and it used to bother me, but I don't care anymore."

Matthew headed out the door. He paused and turned as if to say something. Michelle's tears were now streaming down her cheeks, unstoppable.

"Give my regards to Yannik, will you? Tell him I said thank you for the help."

Matthew dashed out the door and headed for his car; his head felt like it was on fire. As he drove back to the main store, with every second, waiting at every stop sign or traffic light, his heart sank lower and lower into his stomach. As he reached his designated parking spot, he stopped the car and bent his forehead over the steering wheel. The images inside his head started spinning wildly. He opened his eyes and felt the world around go by in slow motion in comparison with the speed of his thoughts. *Recognize the carrots.* Once again, he had allowed himself to focus on a false goal and let the carrot take the place of what was important. He had just managed to hurt Michelle, the true light in his life, and he could only blame himself. The expression on her face as the tears ran down her pale cheeks was something he couldn't easily forget. In one clear sweeping wave of emotion, Matthew could see and feel the priorities in his life fall neatly into their right slots. There was Michelle, and their bond of love and trust, and all the rest fell far into the distant background. Matthew reached for his cell phone. Just a few weeks ago, the idea of making this call would have seemed unthinkable. He would have thought of himself as a wimp, a weakling. Today, however, Matthew thought of himself as a man, stepping forward into his own shape of success.

"Charles?" he said. "This is Matthew. Can you talk for a minute?"

CHAPTER TEN

CHARLES HAD BEEN SITTING ON THE PATIO WITH CLYDE
having a cup of coffee when the phone rang. He motioned for
Clyde to follow him inside and took Matthew's phone call in
the library, where he could hear him better. Clyde settled in
an armchair and flipped through a magazine.

"Clyde's here with me," Charles said. "You remember
my buddy Clyde, the one who originally taught me the four
truths?"

"Of course," Matthew said. "You can put me on the
speakerphone if you want."

"Yes, if you don't mind?" Charles said.

"You said Clyde helped you in the past, and I certainly
need all the help I can get," Matthew said.

Charles pressed the speakerphone button on his desktop phone.

"Can you hear us?" Charles asked.

"Yes," Matthew replied. "Hello, Clyde."

"Hi, there," Clyde replied and set the magazine back on the table.

"So what are you guys up to?" Matthew asked.

"When we're not playing golf, we're talking golf," Clyde said. "We're organizing a charity fund-raiser for the youth group at our church. Do you play, Matthew?"

"Not really," Matthew said. "It's too sedate for me. But I'll be happy to help cook hamburgers or whatever you do at fund-raisers."

"Fantastic. You're in," Clyde said.

"Matthew wants to tell us about something," Charles explained to Clyde. "He said he needs some help, which, if I may say so, is very good to hear."

"What's good to hear?" Clyde chided. "That he needs help?"

"No!" Charles said. "I didn't mean it that way. I mean it's very good to hear that Matthew thinks of calling me, that he thinks I might help. It's good."

"Thanks," Matthew said, "I appreciate that you take the time to hear all my whining. Let me tell you about my wonderful morning."

Matthew related word by word the phone call from the

reporter, and how someone had eavesdropped and reported the private conversation between Matthew and Charles.

"That's a fairly bad morning," said Clyde. "I'll have to agree with you there."

Charles was silent for a moment.

"Do you have any idea who overheard our conversation?" Charles asked. "Did Brighton give any clues?"

"He wouldn't say anything," Matthew said. "He protects his sources. But I have a pretty firm idea of the culprit."

Leaning slightly forward with both hands gripping the handset, Charles waited.

"It's got to be Yannik," Charles said, "the little snitch."

"Wow," Matthew said, "I think the same, but I wouldn't have guessed that you'd agree with me."

"Who else?" Charles asked. "He was downstairs all the time when we were talking in the bookstore. Little snoop."

"I thought you liked Yannik," Matthew said with surprise.

"Never trusted him," Charles said. "He's the kind of guy who always says what he thinks you want to hear. Too smooth for me. I'd rather have a bit of a rough word or two with a guy, where at least I know where I stand. Like with you. We've been through a few bumps, but you're a man I can talk to."

"I appreciate that," Matthew said.

"Matthew?" Clyde asked. "Did you say Brighton mentioned Seven Seas?"

"He just said that some people have the opposite problem to me," Matthew said, "trying to get out of their lease, and he mentioned Seven Seas. Why, do you know them?"

"Of course I know them," Clyde said, "and I think you know them too. Seven Seas is the corporate name for the owners of the Morton's Arts and Crafts stores."

"Morton's!" Charles said arching his eyebrows.

"It doesn't make any sense!" Matthew said. "Morton's is a classic. I always thought they were hugely successful. Why would they want to leave such a prime location?"

"They are successful," Clyde said, "but I think I may know the reason. The Morton family is from my church. Derek Morton runs the business; he took it over from his father a few years ago. His wife is a scientist, and she got offered an incredible position to do research at Harvard. Apparently it's a very prestigious posting. Last time we spoke, the Mortons were struggling with the decision, but it sounds like they've made up their minds, from what Brighton said."

"Matthew," Charles said, "wouldn't that be a perfect location for you?"

"Beyond perfect," Matthew said, "but I don't put much trust in anything that Brighton says; he's a flake."

"Do you mind if I ask Derek Morton on your behalf?" Clyde asked.

"Of course I don't mind," Matthew said. "That's really generous of you, Clyde."

"What can I say?" Clyde chuckled. "I'm a giving kind of guy."

Charles laughed. "You'll give him a big head. I can picture it swelling already."

"You know what?" Matthew said. "I'm so excited that I'm almost ready to forgive that skunk of a reporter."

"Well, let's see if there's any truth in it," Clyde said. "I'll let you know as soon as I've talked to Derek."

"I'll give you a call later, Matthew," Charles said. "I'm meeting Michelle for lunch. She said she needed to talk. She sounded upset."

"Err . . ." Matthew hesitated, "I know why she's upset. Would you do me a favor, Charles?"

"What's that?" Charles asked.

"Do you mind if I pick up Michelle for lunch instead?" Matthew said. "I need to apologize for something I said."

"Absolutely," Charles said. "We said we'd meet at noon at the IHOP."

"Great," Matthew said. "I appreciate it. Talk to you later then."

After Matthew had hung up, Charles rubbed his temples slowly, looking down at the phone.

"What's the matter, Charles?" Clyde asked. "Is something bothering you?"

"Do you also read minds now?" Charles said with a smile.

"I've known you for over thirty years," Clyde said, smiling back.

"I was wrong about that young man," Charles said.

"Who, Yannik?" Clyde asked.

"No, not Yannik. I've always known there was something too good to be true about Yannik," replied Charles. "I mean Matthew. He seems to be a really good kid. God has truly turned his heart around."

"And your heart too," Clyde said.

"Yes," Charles said, "but I've said terrible things about him, and I really snubbed him at the party after what that Brighton vulture published in his article. I wish I could take those words back."

Clyde reflected for a moment.

"Are you meeting him soon for one of your chats?" he finally asked.

"Yes," Charles said, "this afternoon actually."

"Then tell him how you feel," Clyde said. "Start your meeting by coming clean and asking for his forgiveness. Simple."

"Yes," Charles said, "quite simple."

Clyde nodded. "There is no need to carry this burden on your shoulders anymore," he said, "and make him carry it around as well. Get it all out in the open and be done with it. God is waiting for you to give it all up to Him. He won't let you fall. Who knows what wonderful blessings you've missed in your life because you have been holding on to your attitude about this kid? Think of what's at stake. He may be a member of your family soon, and possibly he'll become the most important factor in your daughter's future happiness. What could be more worthwhile?"

Charles got up and headed back out to the patio. He paced back and forth, picking up their coffee mugs and taking them back into the kitchen. Clyde followed him inside.

"I have so many blessings in my life, Clyde," Charles said, "and your friendship is one of the biggest of all."

"Then it's time to let this new blessing of Matthew into your life with an open heart," Clyde said, with his hand lightly on Charles's shoulder.

"You're right," Charles nodded and punched Clyde playfully in the arm. "That's what is so irritating about you. You're always right!"

CHAPTER ELEVEN

MATTHEW HAD SECOND THOUGHTS ON THE BRILLIANCE of his idea to surprise Michelle at lunch. He stood by the door of the IHOP restaurant holding a bouquet of coral pink roses with a bag of M&M's candy attached to the bow. This was their private code, shorthand for Matthew & Michelle. Wearing a guilty, sheepish grin, Matthew hoped that Michelle would accept the gesture and even possibly forget that the argument had ever happened. Matthew saw her before she saw him. Michelle stopped for a moment before crossing the street to retie her ponytail, allowing her golden hair to blow in the wind before wrapping it again. Matthew waved the flowers. From across the street Michelle's eyes drilled into him with such truth that it made his chest hurt. She strode across the street and paused a few feet away from him.

"Surprise!" said Matthew.

"So it's true then," Michelle said with arms crossed.

"What is?" he asked.

"What they say about guilty boyfriends and flowers," she said.

"What do they say?"

"You know," Michelle said with a hint of sarcasm, "that when a boyfriend gives you flowers and it's not a special occasion, it's usually a sign of a guilty conscience."

"Not true," Matthew said. "Well, maybe today it applies, but I've given you flowers many other times."

"But it was always for a special occasion," Michelle said, "like my birthday or Valentine's Day. But today is just a regular day," she said, looking toward the door.

"Anyway, I'm meeting up with my dad for lunch."

"I know," Matthew said. "I'm afraid it was a conspiracy. I asked him if I could take his place, and he agreed."

Michelle looked up with a start.

"You talked to my father?"

"Yep," Matthew said. "Listen, babe, about everything I said earlier today. I am so sorry; it was hurtful and insensitive, and I didn't mean a word of it."

"*How* sorry?" Michelle asked playfully, with the hint of a smile forming at the corner of her mouth.

"Infinitely," he said.

"Are those M&M's?" Michelle asked as she reached out for the flowers.

Matthew grasped her hand and pulled her into his arms, and she lifted her head and offered her brightest smile.

"Hungry?" he asked.

"Starving."

They both went through the door, arms tightly wrapped around each other's waist. Matthew felt that his life had turned to pure gold. His misgivings about the business, the odious reporter, and his landlord, all washed away from him in a tide of pure contentment. He had Michelle at his side, and her family was coming to accept him, especially her father. After all that had gone on between them, it was no minor miracle that their relationship had been repaired through Charles's mentorship and Matthew's willingness to listen.

After lunch Matthew had to carry out the unpleasant task of driving by the Velez store to finish checking the final inventory to make sure all his stuff was packed and ready for the movers. It felt like having to throw away the food that had been cooking for days for a party that got cancelled. But in his present mood, Matthew could face anything. Michelle offered her moral support, so they drove together to the store.

"Okay," Michelle said, taking charge. "Let's split the list. I'll do this page, and you do that one. Mark the boxes that you've checked and we'll be out of here in no time."

Michelle knew that Matthew wanted to get it done as quickly as possible. They started working their way through the boxes. As they were just finishing, they heard a key in the door, and a lady entered, armed with a photo camera and notepad. Matthew could not imagine that a journalist would be interested in their task today, not even someone working for Brighton. Besides, a reporter wouldn't have a key. It had to be Mrs. Velez. The lady shot an awkward glance toward them and hesitated. She then walked toward the back of the store to where they were working.

"Hello," Matthew said, offering his hand. "Are you Mrs. Velez by any chance?"

"Yes, hello," she said.

Matthew introduced himself and Michelle.

"We'll be out of your way as quickly as possible," Matthew said.

"No need," Mrs. Velez said, softening her expression slightly. "I can come back later."

"Absolutely not, we are almost done," Matthew said. "Michelle helped me with the list, and we are just about ready. We're just checking that everything is ready for the movers."

"I see," Mrs. Velez said. "You sell mattresses?"

"Yes," Matthew said, as Michelle handed Mrs. Velez a catalogue from one of the boxes. "We like to think that we sell 'sleep improvement' solutions."

Mrs. Velez smiled and looked at the catalogue.

"These are really nice," she said. "I suppose we do spend a good many hours in our beds, don't we?"

"About a third of our lives," Matthew said. "It makes a difference when you have a comfortable and healthy environment to get your rest."

"My sister has an interior decorating store," Mrs. Velez said. "You've probably seen it, at the entrance of the mall."

"Oh yes," Michelle said. "They have beautiful things there. I often stop to daydream at the window!"

"I wonder if she's ever thought of having an Easy Mattress section there. It would fit very well. I'll tell her to give you a call," Mrs. Velez said, her smile widening. "I'll let you continue with your work; don't let me interrupt you."

Mrs. Velez returned to the front of the store and made herself busy taking notes. After a few minutes, Matthew and Michelle had finished their checklist and walked up to the door.

"Well, we're done," Michelle said. "It was a pleasure to meet you."

"I wish it was under different circumstances," said Mrs. Velez.

"Oh, don't worry about it," Matthew said. "There are worse things in life."

Mrs. Velez nodded. "I know, like a divorce, for example." She paused briefly before continuing. "Can I ask you something? How did you know who I was?"

Matthew smiled. "Well, it was a hunch. You had a key, and you acted like you owned the place."

"Did I?" Mrs. Velez said, blushing. "I didn't mean to cause any inconvenience, you know."

"I know," said Matthew. "Besides, I cheated. I had seen a photo of you before. Your wedding picture in the office."

"That thing is still there?" Mrs. Velez asked.

"Yes," Matthew said. "And you both look really great in it."

"Well, things have changed since that picture. One hopes for the best, but then reality strikes."

"Maybe things haven't changed that much," Matthew said. "Maybe the important things just get pushed aside, locked up in the back."

Mrs. Velez looked down, as if reflecting on what Matthew had said.

"It's like getting older," Matthew continued. "The mirror shows you an image of what you look like outside, but inside you still feel the way you did when you were twenty."

"I have to agree with that," Mrs. Velez nodded, and when she looked up, her eyes were watering. "Are you two married?"

"No!" Michelle said, before Matthew could respond.

He shot a sideways glance at her.

"I hope you're successful when you are," Mrs. Velez said.

"Thank you," Michelle responded.

"When you get married, you want it to be forever," Mrs. Velez said.

"Of course," Michelle said, reaching out to touch Mrs. Velez's hand.

"It looks to me like you've found a fine man," Mrs. Velez whispered under her breath, and squeezed her hand.

Michelle nodded.

Once they were back in the car, a long silence followed as Michelle and Matthew said their silent farewells to the hope of the new store.

Michelle was the first to interrupt the silence. "That's interesting, what Mrs. Velez said."

"About me being such a fine man?" Matthew smiled.

"You heard that?" Michelle teased. "No, I mean what she said about her sister's store. Having an Easy Mattress section inside a big interior decorating store."

"Yes, true," Matthew said, starting the car. "I never thought about it that way. It almost sounds like a micro-franchise system. Interesting. Mrs. Velez seems to have a good head for business."

"What a shame about the divorce. They both seem like such nice people," Michelle said.

"Yes," Matthew said. "A real shame."

CHAPTER TWELVE

THIS GLOW FROM SPENDING TIME WITH MICHELLE stayed with Matthew throughout the afternoon, all the way to the time of his meeting with Charles. After the fiasco of the overheard conversation at the bookstore, they decided to meet up at Matthew's original store in the privacy of his office. Charles arrived right on time.

"I'm very impressed, Matthew," Charles said, settling into the visitor chair across from Matthew's desk. "This is a fine store."

"You're generous," Matthew said. "It's just mattresses, not exactly a revolution in the market."

"But you've presented your product very well," Charles

said. "In fact, it looks so nice that it made me think that we might need to change our mattress! I'm under the spell!"

"We strive to serve . . . and to hypnotize our customers to happily part with their money," Matthew said, laughing.

It struck Matthew as slightly odd to meet Charles in home territory. He tried to make Charles feel at ease. He could sense that he was a little more reserved than usual.

"So why did you pick mattresses?" Charles asked. "Such a departure from your previous line of business."

"Well," Matthew said, "I knew absolutely nothing about bedding or mattresses or anything related to home furnishings, so it seemed like a perfectly logical progression."

Charles laughed and seemed to relax.

"No, seriously," Matthew continued, "it was simply an article I read in a magazine in my dentist's waiting room. It showed a statistic about how often people need a new mattress and how hard it is to choose the right one; it grabbed my attention. Plus, I can remember going shopping for a mattress, and it was always a hassle. Too many choices and too long to wait for delivery. Plus, every time I would go in a store that would have forty mattresses to choose from, the salesperson would always take me to a specific group of two or three mattresses and say that 90 percent of their sales were generated from just those three. So, why stock the other thirty-seven and have all that overhead? I like the idea of keeping it simple for the customer and making the mattress available on the same day. Our small store size allows us to keep our prices down. Customers love the convenience."

"You seem to have an instinct for it," Charles said. "This store is doing well?"

"Very well," Matthew said. "This false start with the new branch gave us a bit of a headache, but we'll recover. By the way, have you heard back from Clyde about the Seven Seas people?"

"Not yet," Charles said, "but it's only been a few hours."

Matthew smiled. "I know. Patience is not my strong point. But I'm really learning not to chase carrots. Actually what you said the other day made a lot of sense to me."

Matthew related how he had experienced moments during the past week where he caught himself in the "pigpen" and how he had been able to adjust his course back to God's way.

"I'm looking forward to Truth Number Three," Matthew said. "The first two were so helpful."

"Before we get into that," Charles said, "there's something I would like to say to you. This is hard for me, so I hope it comes out right."

Matthew poured two glasses of mineral water and waited for Charles to continue.

"Please forgive me," Charles said.

Matthew froze in his seat, unsure if he had heard right.

"Forgive you?" Matthew said. "For what? I thought it was the other way around."

"Well," Charles said, "there's a lot you don't know. After

we had our falling out, I spent years bad-mouthing you, and I harbored a lot of resentment. Besides, as you are well aware, I even cooperated with Brian Brighton and fed him all that baloney about your unethical business practices."

"Oh, Charles," Matthew said. "I'm not sure we should even go there. It's all in the past, and there's so much for us in the future."

"I agree with you," Charles said. "That's exactly the way I feel. But I still need to know that you forgive me."

"Don't worry about it." Matthew swept his hand over his shoulder. "It's all in the past."

"Do you forgive me?" Charles asked again. "I need to hear those words."

"This is officially awkward," Matthew smiled. "Charles, I forgive you."

"Good," Charles said letting out a deep sigh. "That's good. That's really good. So let's get on with it. Where were we?"

"Truth Number Three?" said Matthew, relieved.

"Ah, yes," Charles said. "I must go back to the root of that awkward moment we just had to explain this one."

"Oh no!" Matthew smiled.

"I'll keep it brief," Charles chuckled. "It was at the time when our differences were going on. Let's just say that my affections for you were at their all-time low."

Matthew nodded.

"As I said, even my family was tired of hearing it," Charles continued. "My world had started to quickly close in

on me. I found myself reading Ephesians 3:20, which basically says that God is capable of doing more than we can ever
imagine. I tried to imagine the solutions to my problem,
praying for God to open a door for me. I remember I would
ask for a different thing each day, as I kept refining my idea
of the perfect solution. I would ask God to help you lighten
up and see what you were doing, or I would ask God to bring
me another customer to replace the profits I was forfeiting
through your company's abusive demands on us. Finally,
when I was fresh out of original ideas, I just prayed. I asked
God for His favor."

"So what happened?" Matthew asked.

"There's no nice way of saying this," Charles said, "so
I'll just say it. You got fired from your own company."

Matthew struggled against the old feelings welling up to
the surface. He attempted to regain his focus on what Charles
was saying.

"Do you mean to say that I got sacked in answer to your
prayers?" Matthew said.

"I guess I'm trying, very inarticulately, to get to Truth
Number Three, and that is to really believe and act like God
can do more than we can imagine. In short, we must not try
to put God in a box. Most people know this to be true, they'll
say God can do anything, but you rarely see people acting
like they truly believe what they are saying. Most people,
including myself before I found this truth, continue to limit
God to the box of what they hope God *might* do. I would

have never, in a million years, have thought of asking God to kick you out of your company, because I wouldn't have been able to conceive that possibility in my mind. But it happened, and God became more real to me than ever before. I'm sorry if this is uncomfortable for you to hear, Matthew, but it needs to be said if I am to be a truthful witness of my own experience."

TRUTH #3
We must not try to put God in a box.

Matthew nodded, much slower this time.

"From that point on," Charles continued, "I have always operated my business and lived my life in such a way so as not to put any of my own limitations on what I expect from God. I have to tell you, it's been a great ride ever since. I simply turn matters over to God through prayer and trust that God's will will be done. I get a great sense of peace, and it has helped my professional life and most certainly has helped my family life."

How am I supposed to feel about this? Matthew thought. *What do I say next?* He contained the flush of emotion rising from the idea of Charles seeing his failure as a God-given blessing for himself. He didn't want Charles to be the enemy, not again. He felt Charles's eyes on him, but he could not meet his gaze. He did not want Charles to see in his eyes what was going through his mind. Finally finding his most neutral voice, Matthew spoke.

"I am going to think this one over," he said. "I appreciate your candidness."

"Right," Charles said, getting up. "I'll leave you to it. Anna must be wondering where I am; we have guests for dinner. I hope I didn't upset you. Are you okay?"

"I'm fine," said Matthew. "You just gave me a lot to think about. I still have some work to do."

"I'll show myself out," Charles said. "See you soon."

"Please give my regards to Anna," Matthew said as Charles closed the door behind him.

Charles made his way through the store and out the main door as a clerk locked the door behind him. In the late twilight a fine drizzle added a chill to the night air. Charles shivered as he started the car. *That did not go as planned*, he thought. He felt confused. He played the conversation back in his head, trying to understand how his good intentions to ask for forgiveness had turned into an unintended attack on Matthew. Here was a young man who had just endured a great deal of bumps in the last three years, and Charles had just rubbed a considerable amount of salt into a raw wound. Charles wondered, would he and Matthew ever be able to make the fresh start they both wanted and needed?

CHAPTER THIRTEEN

MATTHEW STARTED THE NEXT DAY EARLY DEALING WITH a few minor crises at the main store while at the same time trying to reach Mr. Velez to follow up on the moving truck that should have arrived by now but had not shown up yet. He kept getting either a busy signal or the answering machine. After several attempts, Mr. Velez answered his phone.

"Matthew!" Mr. Velez sounded excited. "I have been trying to reach you. I've cancelled the moving truck."

"Why?" Matthew was getting irritated. "We had agreed on early morning. I have my guys waiting to unload on this end."

"I've got news," Mr. Velez said. "It's my wife. She had an accident."

Matthew's stomach tightened.

"Is she hurt?" Matthew asked.

"She's fine," Mr. Velez chuckled. "Not that kind of accident. She went to the store to see for herself that you were clearing out your stuff."

"I know," Matthew said. "I saw her there, we spoke for a moment, but she seemed to be okay. What happened?"

"It must have been after you left then," Mr. Velez continued. "She backed her car into the low retaining wall in the parking lot, and the fender became stuck. She couldn't reverse or pull forward. She called me on my cell phone, and when I got there she was crying with happy tears. She said that it was a sign that she got stuck there, that it was wrong to stop you from opening your store after all your hard work. She didn't mention that she had met you, though."

"Yes," Matthew said, "my girlfriend Michelle was with me. But I don't remember discussing anything particular about the lease. At least I don't think we did. It was mostly a general conversation, you know, about relationships and such things."

"Well, you must have made an impression," Mr. Velez said. "Apparently, while she waited for me to pick her up, she said she felt guilty after staring at your new sign and paint job and boxed-up belongings. Who understands women, huh?"

"Amazing," Matthew agreed.

"So," said Mr. Velez, "what do you say? Do you still want to rent the store?"

Matthew paused. All he could think of was what Charles had said the day before, about Truth Number Three: *We must not try to put God in a box.* He had spent a little extra time in prayer last night before going to bed, mainly focused on asking God to help him to not be angry or bitter toward Charles but to appreciate him. He remembered ending the prayer by telling God that he believed God could do anything, including straightening out his relationship with Charles and providing a good location for his new store.

"Matthew? Are you there?" said Mr. Velez.

"Yes," Matthew answered, "I was just thinking. God does more than we can imagine."

"Pardon?"

"Never mind," said Matthew. "Yes, of course I still want to rent."

"Great," Mr. Velez said, "I'll have my guys unpack and put everything back in place. We'll help you recover lost time. Come by whenever you can, and I'll have the lease ready for you, signed by Mrs. Velez, of course."

Matthew walked out of his office and sat on one of the display beds in the front room. He could not stop shaking his head. Amazing. His cell phone rang, and for an instant he feared it was Mrs. Velez changing her mind again. It was Clyde.

"Hey, Matthew," said Clyde. "I hope you don't mind, Charles gave me your number."

"Of course not, Clyde," Matthew said.

"Good news, my friend," Clyde said. "I spoke to the Seven Seas people and the stores will be available for rent, and you are the first in line if you are interested."

"I don't believe it," Matthew gasped.

"Better believe it because they are expecting you this afternoon," Clyde said. "I hope that's okay. I can meet you there and make the introductions, and then I'll leave you to discuss it. How about three o'clock? Can you make it?"

"Sure," Matthew said. "I'll be there."

"Great! See you then," Clyde said.

Everything had happened so quickly that Matthew forgot to thank Clyde. He just sat there, on the edge of the bed, looking around at his store already busy with customers and staff milling around. He felt like yelping out in joy and crying at the same time. He was back in business. His new store was going to happen after all, and right on schedule. Not only that, but now he had a choice of locations to pick from. Amazing. Matthew kept repeating the word to himself over and over. *Amazing*. He knew what he had to do next. He flipped his cell phone open and dialed.

"Charles? It's Matthew," he said. "You won't believe what happened!"

"Matthew! I'm so glad you called." Charles's voice was that of genuine relief. "I feel so bad for what I said yesterday."

"Forget it," Matthew said. "I confess I was a little miffed, but it's all good. Charles, God can do more than we can imagine, remember?"

"Of course," Charles said. "Truth Number Three. So what's up?"

Matthew told Charles of the two phone calls from Mr. Velez and Clyde. Charles started laughing and couldn't stop. It was contagious, and Matthew started laughing at the same time. He could feel the curious stares from his staff.

"They are true," Matthew finally said. "The truths, they do work."

"Yes," Charles said, "they not only work, they keep surprising me every time, and I'm the one telling them to you! So what are you going to do? Which store are you going to choose?"

"I'll see what happens at the Seven Seas meeting, and then I'll be able to decide. Now I'm spoiled for choice!"

Matthew promised to call Charles and keep him updated.

"One last thing, Matthew," Charles said. "If you don't have any plans for Thanksgiving, we would like you to spend it with us at home. I make a mean stuffing, and Anna makes the best pumpkin pie in the world."

Matthew missed a beat. He couldn't speak. His throat welled up, and no words came. He was overcome by the meaning of such an invitation. Ever since losing his parents, Thanksgiving had not had any place in his life; he had shut it out so as to not feel the pain of their absence. Instead, he could now look forward to Thanksgiving with Michelle and her family, and the image of Christmases, birthday parties, and slow Sunday dinners filled his heart with warmth. How could so much light arrive, after the darkness, all at the same time, taking away every shadow and making everything suddenly so bright?

"Thank you, Charles," Matthew said. "I'd love to."

"Terrific," Charles said, "I'll let you go then. You have a busy day ahead!"

It was indeed a busy day. First, Matthew made a few phone calls, one to Mrs. Velez's lawyer, who confirmed what Mr. Velez had said. The paperwork would be signed and ready for him in the morning. He then met Michelle for lunch to tell her the news. Just to see the genuine happiness on her face almost made the previous heartache worthwhile. Thinking himself the most fortunate man alive, Matthew then drove by the two locations of the Morton's craft stores to refresh his memory as to the characteristics of each. They were both very desirable, even better in many ways than the location of Mr. Velez's store, but Matthew kept himself from getting too excited. There had to be a catch.

But there was no catch; the meeting went smoothly. Clyde was there to meet him and introduce him to Derek Morton, and then Clyde excused himself and left the two men to discuss the details. Derek showed Matthew every inch of the store; then they drove to the other location. Finally, Derek even disclosed some of his financials to give Matthew an idea of how the location had been growing over the years as the adjacent shopping areas grew in size and variety and kept attracting an increasing number of people to the area.

"It has been a great location for us," Derek Morton said, "but it's time to go. There are six months left on our lease that I would have to pay for, so if you take it over you would be doing us a favor. Then you would renew the lease directly with the owner. He's offering you the same lease amount that we were paying, and I have to tell you, it's a very good price."

Derek showed Matthew the copy of the lease agreement. Matthew couldn't believe his eyes.

"Is that what you are paying today?" Matthew asked.

Derek nodded.

"It's not possible," Matthew said. It was the same amount he was paying in his original location, which was not even close to the superior quality of the Morton store.

"I know," Derek said, "but the owner is old-fashioned. He keeps his word and isn't a speculator. He wants to rent his store to someone he can trust, he said. The only thing is that he wants to rent the two locations to the same tenant, so I don't know if that would suit you. Also, please keep it confidential. I wouldn't want to hurt the owner's chances to raise the price if you decide not to take his offer, and he has to find a new tenant."

"I'm sure he would have a long line of candidates," Matthew said.

"He sure would," Derek said, "but it hasn't been advertised yet. As I said, it is a pretty special location, and there will be plenty of interest, so don't worry if you decide it's not for you. No pressure. Think about it, and let me know in a couple of days."

Matthew left the meeting with a lot to think about. He would have to decide whether to stay at Mr. Velez's location or take up the two locations in the Morton lease. But what would he do with two stores? His head was spinning trying to figure out the best decision. As he walked away from the Morton store, Matthew took a deep breath, and a quiet calm fell upon him, like the warm morning sun after a chilly night. He would turn it over to God and follow His wisdom. *God can do more than we can imagine.* Matthew was convinced more than ever that he could not put God in a box.

CHAPTER FOURTEEN

AT DAWN THE NEXT DAY, MATTHEW SAT IN HIS OFFICE running through financial projections for the three possible store locations. Everything was quiet around him, but he found it hard to think. Contrary to most people, he worked best surrounded by bustle and activity. The numbers didn't lie. The main location of the Morton's store was the best possible scenario, but the fact that the two stores were to be leased in tandem inserted a different spin into the equation. Could he stretch to expand into two stores at the same time? Would that be wise? Also, there was Mr. Velez's store to consider. Matthew felt an allegiance to the man, after what he had been through to get his wife to sign the lease. He would have to make his decision quickly as the lease would be ready for him to sign later in the morning. God had indeed provided him with more than he could ever imagine. He had presented him with *too many* choices! Matthew heard a door opening. He was unaware of anyone coming in early that day. It was Dave Hallworth, the store manager.

"Hey, Dave," Matthew called out.

Dave almost jumped back with surprise.

"Didn't mean to startle you," Matthew said. "What are you doing here so early?"

"I'm just catching up on some paperwork before our big sale next week," Dave said. "The inventory went a little crazy with all the stuff going to the new store and now scheduled to come back into this one. Just a few glitches, no worries."

"Well, guess what?" Matthew said. "The inventory may not be coming back after all. Let me show you."

Dave made some coffee, and they both huddled over the figures as Matthew explained to Dave the options that were suddenly available to them. Dave concentrated over the figures, and Matthew felt grateful to have such a trustworthy man on his team. Dave had been with Matthew since day one of the business; he was a young, dependable employee with a family and a dream to start his own business one day.

"So what do you think?" Matthew asked.

Dave scratched his head and arched his eyebrows.

"I don't know, Matthew," Dave said, laughing. "They all look good. Let's open all three!"

"Yeah, right," Matthew laughed. "Let's see how fast we

can bankrupt the place! Break my own record. Give something for Brighton to write about."

There was a silence.

"It would be crazy," Dave said.

"Yes, it would," Matthew responded with squinted eyes.

"Bigger is better, they say," Dave said.

"Sometimes bigger is just bigger," Matthew quipped.

"Donald Trump says, 'Think big or go home,'" Dave teased.

"My banker says, 'Think operating capital or go bust,'" Matthew replied.

"Shame," Dave said.

Matthew nodded. "Yep, opportunities like these don't come every day."

"On the other hand, as my wife would say, this is a high-class problem," Dave said.

"What do you mean?"

"Well," Dave said, "yesterday you didn't have anything. Just a voided lease and a few trucks of merchandise with nowhere to go. That was a problem. This, today, picking the best location out of three, this is a high-class problem."

They both sat in silence for a few minutes. Looking at Dave and knowing of his dream to own his own store someday, Matthew began to form an idea in his head. At first he dismissed it, but the idea kept popping up, claiming a more vivid picture each time. Before Matthew could speak, Dave gave a firm tap on the papers with his pen and broke the silence.

"One question for you."

"I was just about to ask you something too," Matthew said.

"You go first then," Dave replied.

"No, you first," Matthew insisted.

"Right," Dave said. "This may sound weird, and it's none of my business, but have you ever thought of—"

"Franchising?" Matthew finished the sentence.

They both looked at each other and nodded.

"How did you guess?" Dave said.

"Mrs. Velez said something a few days ago that made me think," Matthew said. "Apparently her sister owns that huge interior decorating place in the mall, and Mrs. Velez was thinking out loud. She said that it would be perfect to have an Easy Mattress section inside the store. Made me think of a franchise."

"Sounds like an idea," Dave said.

"Do you think the market would support it?" Matthew asked.

"Let's do the numbers." Dave nodded toward the computer.

Both men worked independently in their offices, comparing notes every half hour, and then going back to their own feasibility figures and best- and worst-case scenarios for each franchise and for the parent company. Three hours later, Matthew phoned Charles.

"Charles," Matthew said, "you won't believe the shape

things are taking."

Matthew gave Charles a brief summary of the latest idea.

"It's getting pretty intense," Matthew concluded.

"It's quite a ride when you accept that God can do more than you can imagine, isn't it?" Charles said and chuckled.

They agreed to meet at the coffee shop. When Charles arrived, Matthew and Michelle were already there. Through the shop window Charles could see the couple, huddled over the table, smiling. Matthew said something, and Michelle's hair flew over her face as she doubled over with laughter. Charles felt a wave of warmth flow up into his heart; how he loved to see his daughter laugh like that. He remembered the early days of his own relationship with Anna, how they would get into arguments over small things. Over the years, they had learned to bring God into their family, the value of harmony, and that each day was too precious to waste by spending it in negative moods. He thought back to the time when he had allowed himself to fall into the pigpen, taking his business troubles home and spoiling the harmony they had built with so much care. Charles remembered the first time Michelle had brought Matthew home, and marveled at how his feelings had changed. As a protective father, he had always felt that there wasn't any man nearly good enough for his daughter. Now he realized that Michelle was perfectly capable of finding her own happiness, and with his stubborn ways, he had almost made a mess of it. He offered a silent prayer that Matthew would truly forgive his harsh words and his untimely judgment of character. Michelle waved when she spotted her father walking through the door.

"There you are!" she said, and gave him a hug.

Charles felt his cheeks flush with joy.

"We were discussing this franchising idea," Michelle said. "Isn't it exciting? Maybe one day I can franchise my bookstore."

"Bibles 'R' Us," Charles laughed, stroking his daughter's hand.

"Hmmm," Matthew said, "there's a thought."

"Maybe not," Michelle said.

"Why not?" Matthew asked.

"Well, for one thing, I'm not planning to have the bookstore forever."

"You're not?" Charles asked, surprised.

"I don't have any plans to quit." Michelle's cheeks went crimson. "But if I ever . . . you know . . ."

"What?" Charles asked.

"Start a family," Michelle said. "Not right now, I mean, but . . ."

She looked across the table at Matthew, but he avoided her gaze. Michelle's brow wrinkled.

"I'd better go," Michelle said. "Yannik is coming to the bookstore for the handover to the new intern."

"Is Yannik leaving?" Matthew asked.

"Yes," Michelle said, gathering her handbag. "We had a talk the other day, and he said that he's almost due for his dissertation and has to dedicate his full attention to it, so I found another student, Rachel. She's starting today."

As Michelle left, Charles changed chairs to sit across from Matthew.

"Do you think Michelle asked Yannik to leave," Matthew asked, "after he ratted off to Brighton?"

"I think he probably took a hint," Charles said. "She probably didn't even have to ask. That would be my guess. Not that you'll be sorry to see the back of him."

"No," Matthew said with a thin smile, "he won't be missed."

"So how about the franchising idea?" Charles said.

"What do you think?" Matthew asked. "Am I hallucinating? When I was talking to Dave this morning, it almost felt as if the idea was being whispered into my ear. I admit I had considered the possibilities of franchising in my early business planning, but penciled it in as something to look at years down the road. Now, everything is happening so quickly that my head is starting to spin. I'm so excited and scared at the same time."

"I know the feeling," Charles said.

"The best part is that Dave wants to be a franchisee," Matthew said, "which is great because he deserves it, and I know he's always wanted to start his own business. But it's scary at the same time because I know he has two small children, and I would hate for him to suffer any hardship on account of my business decisions. But then I think that I made the right decision not suing Mr. Velez and how that gave way to all these new options opening, so I must be doing something right. It's hard to know which way to go."

"I had something like that happen to me. More than once actually. Do you have time for Truth Number Four?"

"After what happened with the other three truths," Matthew said with a smile, "how could I refuse?"

"It's just that your present situation makes me think that we better go over Truth Number Four right away so you will have all the tools you need. I summarize Truth Number Four as: We must follow God on His plan, not include Him in ours," Charles said.

"I'm all ears," Matthew said, leaning back in his chair.

"This happened quite a few years back," Charles said,

TRUTH #4
We must follow God on His plan,
not include Him in ours.

"right when my business was in a tight crunch and every single order, even the smallest, was a lifeline. We were literally surviving week to week. Our biggest competitor, Joe, was tough and was naturally trying to push us out of his turf. It's the name of the game; I couldn't blame Joe for it. But then one of Joe's biggest clients, a mail-order gift service, suddenly declared bankruptcy. It happened almost overnight.

We were all shocked and congratulated ourselves on our fortunate escape. But that was not all. This client, Baxter, the owner of the mail-order company, had left Joe with huge unpaid invoices. Apparently in his efforts to assert his dominance in the market against us, Joe had taken risks and allowed a longer-than-normal billing cycle with Baxter, it being his biggest client and all. Baxter had wrapped everything into a corporate shield so the bankruptcy couldn't touch most of his assets. In short, Joe's business didn't survive the hit. The bankers zeroed in on him, and he had to close his doors. Joe is a good man, though, and he didn't leave any debts unpaid. He left like a true gentleman. So while Joe lost his business and even his home in the fracas, Baxter still lived in his big mansion, with his two luxury SUVs, protected by the bankruptcy. Anyway, the following year Baxter came back, reincarnated into a new catalog business, like nothing had happened. Joe was out of the picture, so naturally Baxter approached us to be their main vendor."

"Wow!" Matthew said. "So what did you do?"

"At first I was tempted," Charles said, "very tempted. But then I thought of what Baxter had done to Joe. You see, I had always respected Joe. I used to see him at trade events and industry events. He had always impressed me as a straight arrow. We used to have some deep, very personal conversations. I even shared my faith with Joe a couple of times when the opportunity arose. Suddenly, when Baxter came to us, I thought, *What would Joe think if I were to welcome this cus-*

tomer that had injured him so? What would Joe think of me and my faith? He would never want any part of the God I serve, and with good reason. I would be a very poor witness indeed. At the same time, I had the projections for the orders from Baxter in front of me, and I kept trying to ease my conscience by saying that I had nothing to do with Baxter's bankruptcy, and I kept struggling to find a way that I could fit God into my plans. It didn't work. You see, Matthew, it is quite easy to include God in your plans; it is quite another story to *follow* Him where His plans take you. This was a big, juicy carrot dangling in front of my eyes just at the time when our business needed it the most."

"But you couldn't take Baxter on board, could you?" Matthew asked.

"The right path was plain to see, I'm afraid," Charles said. "Even though it would have filled the need for our business in the short term, I knew Joe would find out. I decided to take the high road and trust God."

"Bitter decision," Matthew said.

"Not really," Charles said. "Bitter at the time, but quite sweet in the long run. You see, when I turned down Baxter, it made quite a stir in the market. Joe heard about it, as I knew he would, and guess what he did?"

"He gave you the phone number of the closest asylum?" Matthew teased.

"Not quite," Charles laughed. "It sounded crazy, but of all people, I knew Joe would understand my motivation. He immediately called all his good clients from before and told them what I had done. In a matter of one week all these former clients of Joe's started placing orders with us. I had more work than I could handle. We started gradually expanding our operation and, what's more important, every single one of those clients that Joe referred to me is still doing business with us today."

"Amazing," Matthew said. "So what happened with Baxter?"

"The new clients turned out to be ten times better than any business Baxter could have given us," Charles said. "Baxter's catalog business is still going, but they took a long time to get online, and the other Internet businesses gained ground. We ended up ahead with the decision we made."

"So what you are saying," said Matthew, "is that when you were merely including God in your plans you were blinded to the true direction that He was trying to lead you."

"Precisely," Charles said. "The big difference is that following usually requires some sacrifice. To include God was more of a feel-good approach to justify my own agenda. You'll hear a lot of people say that they are following God, but they are not going where God is going; they want to take God where they are going. God has a bigger plan for us. Satan, on the other hand, will try to convince us that including God in our plans is good enough and all that is needed. It is just another of his carrots to distract us from the real plan that God has for us."

"Satan knows how to choose his carrots," Matthew said,

shaking his head.

"As you face many small and large decisions," Charles said, "don't be scared. Pray about them and just follow God's leading, regardless of the business practicality of it all. I tell you, Matthew, the more I experience God over the years, the easier it has become to trust Him. I am at the point now," Charles winked, "where I even believe that God can do things better than I can."

"No way," Matthew laughed. "That's a big admission!"

"It took me awhile to come to that conclusion," Charles laughed back. "Well, I better get to work. Let me know if I can help you with anything."

"One more thing before you go, Charles," Matthew said. "There's something I have to ask you."

"Sure, what is it?" Charles seemed interested.

Matthew took a few sips of coffee and had a fearful look on his face.

"Is something wrong?" Charles acted puzzled, but at the same time seemed to know what was about to follow.

After a few seconds of silence, Matthew smoothed a clean napkin on the table, reached into his pocket, pulled out a small black box, and carefully set it on the napkin. He lifted the top to reveal a gold band with a set of two brilliant, cut diamonds hugging a round, blue sapphire in the center.

"Is that what I think it is?" Charles asked with eyes wide open and a big smile.

Matthew nodded and gripped his knees underneath the

table.

"The big question?" Charles asked, prolonging Matthew's agony.

Matthew nodded again.

"I'm sorry to disappoint you, Matthew . . ." Charles said.

Matthew looked up at Charles with furrowed brow.

"The problem is," said Charles, pointing at his left ring finger, "I'm already married."

They both exploded with laughter, causing stares from the other tables.

"May I have your blessing, Charles?" Matthew asked with relief. "What do you say?"

"I say that my daughter is a very blessed girl. Go to it!"

Without another word, Matthew flew out of the coffee shop, a man on a mission. He drove straight for the bookstore, only stopping at the flower shop to pick up a dozen pink roses, and waited until he saw that there were no clients browsing. He knew this was the right moment, but suddenly his legs were not responding. He couldn't get out of the car. He took three deep breaths and practiced the usual exercise of visualizing the two opposing scenarios. "What is the best thing that could happen?" he asked out loud. Clearly that would be Michelle saying yes and becoming his wife. "What is the worst thing that could happen?" Okay. He decided the exercise wasn't helping. He could hardly think of life without Michelle by his side. He forced himself to jump out of the car and in two strides was inside the bookstore.

"Matthew!" Michelle said with a smile, and then stopped. "Is something wrong?"

"Why?" he said, panting.

"You look like you've seen a ghost," Michelle said.

"I was walking fast," Matthew said and pushed the flowers out in front of him. "These are for you."

"Oh, Matthew! Twice in one week!" Michelle said. "They are so beautiful. Thank you!"

"Can we sit down?" Matthew asked wide-eyed.

"Sure," she said. "Are you sure you're okay?"

"Maybe I need a little help," Matthew said. "I am not doing this very well."

"Doing what?" Michelle asked, as they both sat down at one of the reading tables.

"You know, when we were having lunch today . . ." Matthew said, "and you mentioned something about not keeping the bookstore open in the future in case you ever . . ."

"Started a family?" Michelle smiled. "Didn't mean to scare you. I saw you look down like you wanted the earth to swallow you."

"No!" Matthew jumped. "Quite the opposite, I didn't want to give up my surprise . . . before I talked to your father."

"My father?" Michelle said, and her face became radiant.

Matthew pressed the tiny black box in her hand and bent down on one knee.

"I know it's not the most stable time for me, and I would prefer to have more to offer, everything you deserve, but I love you so deeply, and it feels so right. Would you . . ." he stammered, "w-would you marry me, Michelle?"

Matthew was too nervous to look up into her eyes as he was speaking. When he finally did, all his nervousness washed completely away and melted into a spreading sense of warmth and light.

"Yes!" Michelle cried. "Of course I will!"

Just as she said this, the door chimed, and a group of six teenage girls walked into the bookstore. At first they were chatting among themselves and didn't notice the couple at the table. Then suddenly the girls stopped and looked at the flowers, the ring, and then Matthew and Michelle. One of the girls put her hand on her mouth and looked back at Matthew.

"No way!" she said. "Did you just propose?"

Matthew nodded as Michelle beamed, showing the ring on her finger.

"No way!" the girls squealed. "An engagement! Awesome!"

There was plenty of giggling and hugs as the girls surrounded Michelle, and immediately they started peppering her with questions as the conversation turned to dresses, flowers, how many bridesmaids, morning versus evening weddings, cakes . . . Matthew looked at Michelle as she laughed at the girls' excitement. He felt part of a scene from a storybook. The beautiful maiden surrounded by fluttering fairies. Matthew remembered what Mrs. Velez had said, and how happy she had looked in her wedding photo and how sad she looked now. Matthew made a silent vow to Michelle, to do everything in his power to make sure Michelle would look just as happy twenty or forty years from now as she looked at this very moment.

CHAPTER FIFTEEN

"Hey, future brother-in-law!" Ben waved from the car as Matthew was pulling in behind Michelle's bookstore.

"Hi, Ben." Matthew shook his hand. "How are you doing?"

"Great! I'm home for Thanksgiving for the whole week, so let me know if you need help with the wedding preparations. She said yes, huh?"

"Miracles do happen," Matthew said, as they both walked up to the bookstore.

"No miracle, my man." Ben slapped Matthew on his shoulder. "My sister has always had good taste."

Matthew did a double take. Ben had the rare gift of always saying the words you needed to hear. During the weeks after his engagement he had been in a waking dream wondering how it was possible that so much good fortune had fallen his way. As if he had jinxed it, things at the new stores had started to unravel, and hearing Ben relate to him as part of the family meant that, at least on this aspect of his life, he was doing okay.

"I'm bringing some sample designs for the invitations," Ben said, opening the door. "Apparently Mom is going to make them. When, and if, I ever get married, it will be in a pizzeria with my closest friends and my family. No tuxedo, no frilly cake that nobody likes, just a good, honest pepperoni and double cheese for everybody."

"Hmmm." Michelle laughed as they came in. "How refined. I can't wait."

"I confess I don't understand half of the preparations," Matthew said, hugging Michelle around the waist, "but I just meekly go along."

"Good policy," Michelle said.

Ben set the invitation samples on the counter.

"So when is the big event?" he asked.

"As soon as possible," Michelle replied, looking up at Matthew.

"Michelle wants a Christmas wedding," Matthew said. "Since Clyde's marrying us, we're waiting to hear from him about his schedule to see if it's possible."

"Sounds charming to me," Ben said.

"I want a simple reception," Michelle said. "Not exactly

pizza, but I don't believe in all the theatricals. I'd rather have my friends and family relaxed and enjoying themselves than worrying if their shoes match their dress."

"That's my sister," Ben said, squeezing her shoulders. "I guess I better get home. I have a couple of my friends coming over to watch *Willy Wonka and the Chocolate Factory*. You guys want to come?"

"*Willy Wonka?*" Matthew laughed.

"It's a tradition," Michelle explained. "Always the day before Thanksgiving. Ben has had this ritual with his friends since they were little. Mom makes brownies and chocolate chip cookies, and they drink hot chocolate and roast marshmallows in the fire. It's mostly a sugar rush day."

"*Willy Wonka* rocks," Ben said. "It has a message, you know . . . appreciate the truly important things in life. Are you coming?"

"Tempting," Matthew half-joked, "but I actually have to work late today. I just came to drive Michelle home, but then I'm going back to the store."

Michelle looked away to the side and then started to get ready to lock up.

"Then Michelle can come," Ben said, sensing a change in the mood "Clyde's coming. He loves *Willy Wonka*. Mom and Dad watch it with us too. Plus this year we are watching the new version with Johnny Depp. How about it, sis?"

"I won't fit into my wedding dress if I start eating like

you," Michelle said over her shoulder as she went to the back office to get her coat. "For Ben, the chocolate season starts at Halloween and continues until Valentine's Day."

When Michelle was out of earshot, Ben turned back to Matthew, burying his hands deep in his coat pockets.

"So you're working late, huh?" Ben asked. "Bummer. People are buying too many mattresses?"

"Actually," Matthew said, "the problem is the opposite."

"Uh-oh," Ben asked, almost in a whisper, "is there a secret futon conspiracy?"

"Maybe," Matthew half-smiled, "but we sell futons too, so that wouldn't be a problem. Seriously, though, I haven't got a clue."

Ben leaned back against the counter, pondering.

"Tell me if it's none of my business, but did you tell Dad about it?" Ben asked. "I know the guy wears pleated pants, but don't hold it against him. He does have a good head for business."

"I haven't asked him yet; it's a bit embarrassing," Matthew said. "I thought maybe it was a fluke, because the first few weeks were fantastic. The four stores were running full speed. We had expected the original store to take a hit from the new locations, but, in fact, even that one was doing better than last year. Then it all started to sour, almost overnight. I tell you, it doesn't look good, and if we miss the holiday peak then we'll probably be in serious trouble."

"That stinks," Ben said, and changed the subject as

Michelle came back with her coat and purse. "Maybe we can talk about it with Dad tomorrow," Ben suggested.

Matthew nodded.

"About what?" Michelle asked as she caught the tail end of the conversation.

"Business," Matthew said. "About where on earth our customers are hiding."

"It'll all work out," Michelle said, planting a kiss on Matthew's cheek. "It always does. I'm praying for it."

"I can't imagine how God could ignore the prayers of an angel," Matthew said.

"Enough, you two." Ben grabbed Michelle's elbow. "You need some chocolate, so you're coming with me."

Michelle shrugged, kissed Matthew good-bye, and followed Ben to his car.

"I guess you can't compete with Johnny Depp," Ben called out to Matthew, "but who could?"

Matthew waved good-bye and got back in his car. He didn't like disappointing Michelle. They had planned to look at the invitations together, but it was all he could do to keep from breaking down and screaming. Nothing was making any sense. Everything in the new stores had looked like it was aligned for success. They had carefully analyzed the market, all the numbers were there, the locations were more than perfect. Mrs. Velez herself had surprised him by taking up the first franchise at the Velez location, leasing half of her own store from her husband. The divorce had been put on hold indefinitely, and since then Mr. Velez had a permanent grin stamped on his face, thinking of Matthew as the savior of his family. The original store moved to the first Morton location, the second Morton was franchised to a well-known local businessman with a great reputation, and the third franchise, at the original store location, was operated by Dave Hallworth. The first few weeks had been hectic—but so exciting. The stores had taken off as thoroughbreds right from the start. Matthew had felt so immensely grateful that he wanted to make a gesture to thank God for his prosperity. He had gone the extra mile and decided to offer Sundays to God, to give Him credit for the great gifts of the new locations. He kept the main store closed on Sundays, and encouraged his franchisees to do the same. Mrs. Velez had followed his advice, as did Dave Hallworth, but not before expressing some misgivings as to the wisdom of the decision. But they both owed so much to Matthew for the opportunity that they didn't second-guess his judgment. The other franchisee, Troy Foster, had stayed open but reduced the hours to afternoons only as a way of reaching a compromise. Sundays were usually a big day in the original store, but Matthew had decided to offer this grand gesture to God and trust the results. As Matthew got back to his store, his eyes went up to the sign prominently displayed under the opening hours:

This store is closed on Sundays to allow our employees to spend time with their families and to attend their chosen place

*of worship. For your convenience, our store at 4803 N 12th
Avenue remains open on Sundays from noon to 5:00 p.m.*

Matthew felt a tightness in his stomach. Surely God
would appreciate the sacrifice he was making?

CHAPTER SIXTEEN

THANKSGIVING DAY BROUGHT A GREY, SHRINKING SKY AND a bone-chilling wind that made people rush into doorways hugging their heavy coats. After spending a long, cheerless morning pouring over sales figures in his office, with only a stale bagel to sustain him, Matthew was ready to sit down to a warm meal. As he pulled into the driveway at Charles's house, he noticed Christmas decorations already in the front yard. Matthew rang the bell and waited, rubbing his hands together for warmth.

"Have you decided if you are going to have bridesmaids?" Anna asked Michelle.

"I'm not sure," Michelle said. "I don't want a big entourage."

"Maybe just one maid of honor?" Anna suggested.

"Maybe," Michelle said.

"How about you, Matthew?" Anna asked. "Who's going to be your best man?"

"Let me guess," Charles laughed. "Yannik!"

Matthew laughed without feeling. In all honesty, this had been a matter of some preoccupation to him.

Michelle came to his rescue. "There is a tradition where Matthew comes from in West Tennessee. The role of best man is usually filled by the father of the groom."

A brief silence followed.

"That's so sad," Anna said. "I'm sure you'll find someone special to stand in for your dad."

"I'm sorry your father won't be there to share the day, Matthew," Charles said.

"Thank you, Charles." Matthew nodded. "I miss him. You two would have gotten along very well. He was a decent golfer, my dad."

"So how come you don't play?" Ben chided, rolling his eyes in his father's direction. "I was never given a choice. It was mandatory curriculum."

Matthew smiled. "Maybe I'll try it one day."

Anna took her shoes off and snuggled up on the sofa against Charles's arm, pulling up a knitted throw over her knees, and Charles wrapped his arm around her. It was such a casual gesture, with the ease of affection that flowed between a couple that had managed to keep their relationship fresh over many years.

"I should go," Matthew said. "You must be so tired. The dinner was exquisite."

Anna smiled. "I'm not tired at all. This is my favorite part of every party, mellowing in the afterglow of a full belly. Tell us how the business is going, Matthew. I've been so busy that I haven't even asked you. I had you chopping up salad as soon as you came in!"

"Oh, I don't want to spoil a great evening," Matthew said.

"Go on," Ben encouraged, "there's no ceremony in this house. We just talk about anything anytime. Perfect family chaos. It works."

"Not doing too well then?" Charles asked.

"No." Matthew shook his head. "Not well at all."

Matthew summarized the mysterious absence of customers as he had told Ben the day before. Charles reflected as he absently caressed his wife's shoulder.

"And I assume tomorrow, the day after Thanksgiving, should kick off the peak of the year for you," Charles said.

"Right," Matthew said, "and if it doesn't live up to expectations, then we'll be in deep water."

"And you have no idea what could be wrong?" Charles asked. "No gut feeling?"

"None," Matthew shrugged.

"I'll tell you what," Charles said. "If you're open to it, I can go by each one of the stores over the next few days and see if I can pick up anything that may help."

Matthew perked up a little at the offer. "That would be great, Charles. I appreciate it. I'll come with you, and we can exchange notes."

"Great," Charles said, "then we'll do two stores on Saturday and two on Sunday."

"On Sunday only one store remains open," Matthew said, "but we can schedule the other one for Monday."

"Really?" Charles asked. "Is Sunday a slow day for mattresses?"

"No," Matthew said, "not really. I made the decision to close the main store on Sundays and asked the franchisees to do the same. Dave and Mr. Velez agreed. The other store runs more on a strict business principle, and he said he'd rather open Sundays because all the other stores around him are open. I have to say that he has a point; numbers show that Sunday is his strongest day."

"So why did you make the decision?" Charles asked, although he already knew the answer.

"I felt so grateful to God for all the amazing blessings coming my way," Matthew said. "When I felt that the expansion plans would never happen, God gave me three times more than I ever imagined. So I decided that I would dedicate one big gesture to God, to respect Sundays as His day, and trusted that God would take care of the results."

Charles nodded silently, and Matthew got up and said his

good-byes. He had an early start the next day, although he found it hard to bring such a pleasant evening to an end. Charles showed Matthew to the door. Matthew sensed he had something to say.

"What is it, Charles?" Matthew asked, smiling, as they reached the front door.

"You know me well, now, son," Charles said softly. "It's just that I was thinking about what you said, about closing Sundays. I understand very well your motivation, and I admire you for it. I wish everyone would just close on Sundays; it would make things much easier for everybody, wouldn't it? It would level the playing field, and then everyone could take the day off, and those who wish to worship could do so without having to rush off to their jobs."

"I know," Matthew said, "but unfortunately that's not how it is. Your warehouse is open on Sundays, isn't it?"

"It's essential to meet the shipping deadline on Monday," said Charles.

Matthew arched his eyebrows and shrugged.

"The difference," Charles said, raising his hand as if asking permission to speak, "is that I don't struggle about it. I have thought about the idea of closing on Sundays, but I have never felt a strong burden about it. The warehouse is only open from one to five p.m., and it has never been a problem for us."

Matthew tilted his head to one side, as if he was considering the possibility.

"What prompted you to close on Sundays?" Charles said.

Matthew contemplated Charles's question for a moment. "Well, I guess I felt God wanted me to close on Sundays. I think I expected all my franchisees to follow my lead, but the fact that one store remains open makes it harder on the other three, because now customers expect us to be open. So if they drive up on a Sunday to any of the other stores to pick up their mattress, they find the door closed. I guess the reality of life today is that people are so busy during the week that they use any time they can over the weekend to do their personal shopping. Can't blame them really, but I wish it were otherwise."

Matthew paused again, hesitating.

"Come to think of it," Matthew continued, "if I am completely honest, I was thinking that if I closed the stores out of obedience, then God might do more than I could imagine again and really bless the business with more sales than I could dream possible."

"That was a possibility," Charles said, "but what if the sales are not incredibly high? Would you trust God anyway in that case? You see, you should never expect a programmed result from God, just because you are following Him. If you are following Him for a specific result, that sounds more like speculation. Your motive does not come from your heart. You should follow Him because you love Him, and follow Him wherever He goes. God doesn't put conditions on His love for you."

Matthew nodded. A long pause followed, and Charles opened the door for Matthew and patted his shoulder.

"Look," Charles said, "if you are struggling with this and you feel God leading you this way, then you should obey."

"Even if I'm hurting the business?" Matthew said, almost to himself.

"Hey, it was difficult for me not to expand to Houston, but if I hadn't followed my conviction, I would have been miserable. Time with my family was my thing. Your thing is operating on Sundays. You can pray about it and follow Jesus. It may not be financial results that you get, but you will certainly be blessed."

Matthew had a sleepless night. He woke up at two in the morning, got up to get a glass of water, went back to bed, and woke up again, shivering with cold. He turned up the heating and threw a fleece blanket over the bedspread. The third time he woke up, he went to the kitchen, tore off a piece of paper towel, and wrote something on it. He tucked the paper in his wallet and went back to bed, sleeping soundly until morning. He didn't know it then, but that scratchy writing on a piece of kitchen towel would steer his business back to prosperity.

CHAPTER SEVENTEEN

MATTHEW CLOSED THE DOOR OF HIS OFFICE AND CHECKed his watch again. *Time to go.* He had stopped by on the way to church to check on any last-minute messages. He would be away for two weeks on his honeymoon, the longest he had ever left his business. Dave had offered to supervise his store, so he knew that everything would be under control. He checked his suit, smoothed his tie, and combed his hair one more time. He smiled at his own reflection; he did clean up rather well, he thought. He couldn't wait to see Michelle. As he went out the front door, among cheers from the staff, he glanced at the sign on the door that was now a permanent fixture.

Dear Customer,

The management has allowed us to close on Sundays so that we can spend time with our families and worship as we choose. We apologize if this decision has inconvenienced you in any way. To show you how much we appreciate your visit, please stop by on Monday and we'll give you 10% off your purchase and deliver it to your home for free.

The Staff

Easy Mattress

Ever since he had scribbled that note on that sleepless night of Thanksgiving, the offer for customers to come back on Monday for a discount and free delivery was slowly becoming one of the single greatest word-of-mouth marketing successes in the mattress industry. The reaction from the public had been outstanding. Mondays became the biggest selling day. All the additional sales more than made up for the 10 percent discount. Mr. Velez's truck took care of all the free deliveries centralized from the main store regardless of which store had made the sale, so that the other delivery services would not be overloaded. The system worked like clockwork, and employee morale was high. Matthew had trusted God and had taken a step of faith, without speculation. God did greatly, and now the four stores were working full speed ahead. Even Troy Foster had followed suit and closed his doors on Sundays.

THE CHURCH WAS ONLY A FEW MINUTES AWAY, AND THERE were a few cars already there. The whole town had been covered overnight by a gentle blanket of soft white snow. Matthew recognized Clyde's car and saw the florist and the photographer. He went in through the main door and stopped in his tracks at the scene inside. The church was beautifully decorated for the perfect wedding.

"It must look like this when you arrive at the gates of heaven," Matthew said, shaking Clyde's hand.

"How are you holding up?" Clyde asked. "Nervous?"

"I can't stop grinning," Matthew said.

"You have plenty of reasons to smile, son," Clyde said. "Plenty of reasons!"

Ben, who had been recruited as head usher, looked incredibly dapper in his dark grey suit. He walked up to Matthew with a boutonniere made of a small white rosebud wrapped in a tiny silk ribbon with a single leaf of holly.

"Friend of the bride or the groom?" Ben joked, pinning the flower to Matthew's lapel.

"Particularly good friend of the bride," Matthew replied and gave Ben a brotherly hug, narrowly avoiding a crushed rosebud in the process.

"Everything's ready," Clyde said, "so I'll take Matthew with me until all the guests arrive. We'll wait until you give me the sign."

Ben nodded.

"What's the sign?" Matthew asked.

"When Ben escorts the mother of the bride to her seat, that means that the bride is ready to make her entrance."

"Okay," Matthew said, sticking a finger inside his starched collar, "now I'm officially nervous."

From his vantage point, hidden from view to the right of the altar, Matthew watched the guests arrive and find their seats. He recognized a lot of faces from Charles's office, Charles's golf friends, then Dave, Mr. and Mrs. Velez, and a group of staff from the stores. He had worried, for a moment, that the groom's side of the church would be half-empty, considering that he had no family to contribute to the festivities. To his complete amazement, a large group of people took their seats on his side. He recognized some of the faces, all of Michelle's friends from school, some of them he knew well. They had come with their husbands and some with their small children. It was a beautiful group of young people, the ladies in their silk dresses, and they had graciously balanced the pew population with such grace, as if they had rehearsed this all week. It must have been Ben's doing, Matthew thought. As the minutes stretched, Matthew's heart seemed to be growing bigger than his chest could hold, and, just when he thought he couldn't bear it a moment longer, Ben walked in with Anna on his arm and showed her to her seat in the front pew of the now packed church. This was the sign. Clyde nodded and took his place at the altar, and Matthew stood, hands clasped in front to keep them from shaking. The choir burst into the first chords of "Amazing Grace" and the doors swept open.

Matthew felt his knees sway. There, smiling at him, stood the most beautiful vision he had ever set eyes on. Michelle glided down the aisle, swathed in a simple flowing organza gown, her hair gathered in a soft bun and speckled with fresh white rosebuds matching her bouquet. She floated on the side of her father, who smiled proudly and clasped the hand that Michelle easily rested on his arm. Matthew's feet didn't seem to touch the ground as he stepped forward to receive Michelle's hand when Charles handed her over to him. He shook Charles's hand and took Michelle's tiny gloved fingers in his. The moment they touched, all of Matthew's anxiety left him. Michelle looked poised, smiling, confident of their future together. Clyde looked at Matthew, then at Michelle, and smiled.

"Who gives this woman away?" he asked in a commanding voice.

Charles cleared his throat.

"Her mother and I do," he said.

Then, as they had secretly rehearsed with Matthew the day before (without Michelle's knowledge) Charles stepped back and, instead of walking back to take his place by Anna's side on the front pew, he took two broad steps to the right, taking the position of the best man. An approving murmur rippled through the congregation, as Matthew looked down into Michelle's eyes. Her eyes filled with surprise, then with joy, and then spilled over into one tiny tear that she dried with the back of her white glove.

Anna gently nudged Ben's side and whispered, "Did you know about this?"

Ben discreetly nodded and whispered back, "Who could have imagined, those two getting along, huh?"

EPILOGUE

THE LONG SUMMER SUNSET TURNED THE OUTLINES OF the garden a deep orange gold, and the veranda was opulently perfumed with honeysuckle and jasmine. Anna, Michelle, and Matthew sat in the patio chairs, sipping iced tea and enjoying the first cool breeze of the evening.

"Pity Charles is missing this sunset," Matthew said. "Is he held up at work?"

Anna looked away quickly.

"No," she said, smiling to herself, "he mentioned he had some sort of event. I'm sure he'll tell you all about it later."

"Quick!" Ben cried from the family room. "It's starting!"

Anna rushed to the TV as Michelle pushed Matthew into the room.

"What's starting?" Matthew asked, trying not to spill his iced tea on the carpet.

"Sit here, babe," Michelle said. "It's Brian Brighton's new TV show."

Matthew recoiled as if stung by a swarm of angry bees.

"Oh, no," he said. "I'd sooner have a root canal than watch that viper."

"Shh!" Ben said. "You'll like it. Watch."

Matthew sat obediently, staring at the face of Brian Brighton while the titles of his new TV program rolled. The show was called *Yours Truly Live* to mirror his newspaper column. Brighton, visibly nervous, addressed the camera as he announced the topics of the program and named the guest appearances. To Matthew's astonishment, the list included Mr. Charles White.

Matthew sat mouth agape, frozen in place.

"Surprised?" Ben asked.

"You can say that," Matthew said. "So that's why Charles isn't here."

"Wait till you see this," Ben said.

Brighton made the introduction of three guests, all reputable businessmen from the area, and after a few formalities, addressed the camera directly.

"If you have followed my column," Brighton said with feigned humility, "you will know the indignities that Mr.

Charles White has suffered at the hands of one of the un-
scrupulous young upstarts that plagues our local business
scene. Let me refresh your memories."

Next followed a montage of photos of Matthew's former
business, followed by an unflattering photo of Matthew
shielding his eyes from the flash, all narrated by a voiceover
summarizing the events that led to his business failure. When
the camera went back to the studio, Brighton addressed
Charles directly.

"So, Mr. White," Brighton said, "of all the cruel twists of
life, this man, who almost forced you into bankruptcy, ended
up marrying your daughter. We can only imagine your dis-
tress. How does it feel to have your business nemesis in your
family?"

Matthew stirred in his chair, barely able to keep from
screaming at the TV. Still, he could not peel his eyes away
from the screen.

"Well, Brian," a smiling Charles said, leaning forward,
"we all know that God works in mysterious ways. Let me tell
you what happened."

As Charles spoke, Brighton's face turned from impassive
to pink and then to a very noticeable red. Charles explained
in articulate detail the booming success of Matthew's new
stores, and then went on to talk about how he had found
Matthew to be an outstanding example of a person who
flourishes when given a second chance. He described his
admiration for the way Matthew had taken every blow that

life had thrown at him and had trusted God through his adversity, leading into a bright future.

"God could not have been more generous with my family, Brian," Charles said to an obviously embarrassed Brighton. "So, as you can see, I have not only gained a son, but God has also taught me a valuable life lesson. And we have an opportunity here, through the power of TV, to reach all your readers gathered into one spot. You could benefit from my lesson too, Brian, and admit to your viewers how wrong we both were about our unfair condemnation of a fine young man. I think that would show your true caliber."

Brighton looked at the camera, then back at Charles, and then back at the camera.

"Well," Brighton said quickly, chewing into his words, "we looooove happy endings, don't we? If you are listening, Matthew . . . I'm happy things turned out well for you, and we'll be honored to have you as a guest on one of our shows. Now we'll quickly go to a commercial, and we'll be back in a few moments with more of Yours Truly. We'll be right back."

Anna broke into laughter first, followed by everyone else with clapping and high fives for added celebration. Matthew couldn't believe his ears. This was more than he could have ever hoped for.

With tears of laughter in his eyes, Matthew asked, "How did Charles manage this?"

"It was almost five months ago, just after the wedding," Anna said. "You were on your honeymoon, and Brighton called to ask him to participate in his first panel. He said that you would be one of the topics, and that Charles would have an opportunity to vent his frustration as a cautionary tale for other business upstarts like you. It was like a gift had fallen on Charles's lap. Charles kept saying he never could have dreamed of the opportunity of getting to speak to all Brighton's loyal readers and viewers. He was so excited to be able to straighten the record on how he felt about you."

Just then the commercials ended, and Brighton was back on the screen, but this time there was a notable absence on the panel.

"I guess that was the end of Charles's TV career!" Anna gasped with laughter again.

"That was a surreal moment," Matthew said, shaking his head and smiling. "We couldn't have asked for a better opportunity."

"It was so funny," Anna said. "Charles found it so hard to keep it a secret. He was bursting to tell you, but he wanted it to be a surprise."

Matthew looked at Michelle, and she nodded.

"Well," Matthew said, "he's not the only one with a surprise."

Anna and Ben both turned and looked at Matthew and then at Michelle.

"Are you . . . ?"

Michelle nodded meaningfully.

Anna let out a little happy yelp and hugged Michelle and Matthew.

"I can't wait to see Charles's face!" Anna said, as Ben came and joined in the hug. "God really can do more than we can imagine!"

ACKNOWLEDGMENTS

FROM TODD HOPKINS

To my wife, Michelle, who has supported me in everything and provided great feedback on book ideas while patiently listening to mine.

To my boys, James, Sam, and Matthew. Thanks for praying for me and asking God to use this book in a great way. Your prayers have made a difference!

Sylvia Edwards Davis for your creative ideas and writing.

John McBeath, Bill Lewis, Blake Clements, Stan Carver, Gary and Robin Duncan, and Jim Harris for reading the early manuscript and providing good feedback and ideas.

Mrs. Barb Wagner for proofing the manuscript and reminding me of good, basic use of grammar.

Doris Michaels and Delia Fakis of DSM Agency in New York City for all your good work behind the scenes.

John Hamilton for the initial cover design, and Carrot Chaser artwork.

Doug Jolly and Red Iron Design for book layout.

Pastor John Spencer from Calvary Chapel Gulf Breeze for teaching the Word faithfully.

To Pastor Gary Stump who gave me permission to use his powerful prison ministry story in Chapter Four.

My parents, James and Sheila Hopkins, and my brother, Troy. Thanks for all your support and encouragement over the years.

To my CBMC brothers. Thanks for all your prayers and accountability over the years.

To the Office Pride corporate staff, area developers, and franchisees. Your energy, enthusiasm, and dreams are a great encouragement to me. Stay focused!

To all the mentors I have had in my life, past and present. Thanks for investing in me and helping me to stay on path!

Ray Hilbert for teaming up with me on this and other projects.

To my Lord and Savior Jesus Christ. May You receive all the glory!

FROM RAY HILBERT

First, to my Lord and Savior Jesus Christ, to whom I owe everything, thank You for your grace and mercy with me, particularly in terms of all the "carrots" I chase in my own life.

To my wife and life partner, Beth, I love you, and I am so grateful for your patience with me—especially during the long nights at the computer!

To Andrew James Hilbert, you indeed are a "mighty man of God." Always trust the Lord, always follow His ways, live and lead with integrity!

To Mackenzie Rae Hilbert, you will never be too big or too old to be "daddy's little girl." Indeed the Lord has incredible plans for you. Your heart is tender and beautiful—your smile makes my day. Remain true to what you have been taught— never stray from God's Word that you love to read so much.

To Brooke Renae Hilbert, without question you are a joy. Just being with you makes the whole world okay. Your laughter and expressions absolutely are a gift from God. Always know how precious you are to our Lord, and to your mother and me. You are God's precious child, and may you always trust Him at His Word and never allow anyone or anything to tell you otherwise.
Mom and Dad, thank you for all you have done in my life-

and for trusting God in your life too.

To the incredible Truth@Work staff and board, thank you for allowing me the opportunity to work on these book projects and speak across the country: Matt, Bob, Perry, Scott, Cindy, Toby, Mark, Chuck and Chuck, Pam, Lloyd, Jim, Mo, and all the rest—you are all the best, and I am so grateful you are in my life!

To every Truth@Work member, past, present, and future, thank you for living out your faith at home and in the marketplace—together we can make a difference in the world! Thank you to every follower of Christ who is living out their faith each day at work and at home.

Tom Dafnos, what can I say? Thank you for everything! You have been a friend and encouragement far beyond anything I could have hoped or imagined.

Larry Rottmeyer, thank you for always inspiring me to a new level.

Mark Cress, you are a true friend and mentor. Thank you so much for everything!

Matt Peelen, thank you for your tireless effort and for your never-ending friendship.

To Doris Michaels and her team, once again thank you for your incredible support of our project. We could not have done it without you.

Todd Hopkins, it is an incredible blessing having you in my life, and I am so grateful God has brought us together.

To all the "carrot chasers" out there—as a fellow chaser, thank you for reading this book. I pray we will all pursue God's agenda, not our own.

ABOUT THE AUTHORS

TODD HOPKINS

Todd Hopkins is the Founder and CEO of Office Pride Commercial Cleaning Services, which has its corporate office in Franklin, Indiana. Todd founded Office Pride, an award winning commercial cleaning franchising company, in 1992. Currently, Office Pride has nationwide franchise locations, and provides cleaning services to thousands of buildings.

Todd earned his BBA degree from the University of Memphis and his MBA from Butler University. Todd is also a graduate of the MIT Birthing of Giants Executive Entrepreneur Leadership program.

Through CBMC (Connecting Businessmen to Christ) in Pensacola, Todd organizes and leads men's Bible study groups aimed at helping equip men to live and share the Good News of Jesus Christ in the marketplace.

Todd and his wife Michelle have three boys; James, Sam and Matthew. They live in Pensacola, Florida. Todd and his family attend Calvary Chapel in Gulf Breeze, Florida.

RAY HILBERT

Ray Hilbert is the CEO and Co-Founder of TRUTH @ WORK, a not-for-profit organization based in Indianapolis, Indiana that specializes in working with business owners and leaders helping them build and operate their businesses on proven biblical principles. He travels across America speaking to organizations and churches-equipping people to serve God in and through their work.

Previously, Ray was a Regional Director for Promise Keepers, the nationally known men's ministry, where he facilitated large conferences of 60,000 and developed training programs for churches and other ministries.

He is a graduate of Anderson University in Anderson, IN, where he majored in Marketing and Business.

Ray developed "The Legacy Leadership Coaching System™, which has been utilized by several corporations in the development of their leadership/executive teams. This practical, simple, and effective 1- year Leadership/Coaching system has been a powerful tool for many clients. He is in high demand as a speaker for both corporate and church events.

Ray and his wife, Beth, reside in Indianapolis with their son and two daughters. They are involved with several other religious and business organizations.

For information on scheduling

Todd Hopkins or Ray Hilbert
to speak at your event,
please contact the authors at

www.legacycoaching.com
or through the

Truth@Work or Office Pride
organizations.

WWW.TRUTHATWORK.ORG

The mission of
Truth@Work
is to change the way
America
works by bringing the good news of
Jesus Christ
to the marketplace.

Truth@Work
equips today's leaders to impact the
marketplace for Christ.

To contact Ray Hilbert and find out more about how
Truth@work helps Christian business owners and
leaders, please call:
317-842-1694
or visit
www.truthatwork.org